If we discover, in Heaven, an extended Hebrews 11 "Faith Hall of Fame," I fully expect Joni Eareckson Tada to be on the list. Joni and Friends' new book, *Real Families, Real Needs*, is an amazing source of strength, wisdom, and encouragement for families living with disability.

KIRK CAMERON

Actor, producer, and cofounder of Camp Firefly, a camp for seriously ill children and their families

Real Families, Real Needs accomplishes what very few books for families of kids with special needs have done before: It addresses the needs of all family members who love a child with special needs. The first four sections of the book speak specifically to the unique needs of dads, moms, siblings, and grandparents. The final section helps parents become effective advocates and provides ideas others can employ to support parents and families. With wisdom founded in experience, the authors speak directly to the hearts of family members and meet them at their points of need. I highly recommend it!

JOLENE PHILO

Author of *A Different Dream for My Child* and parent of a child with special needs

As a parent to kids with disabilities, I'm not interested in "all roses" stories that gloss over challenges. This book doesn't do that. Rarely have I come across accounts from real families encompassing the difficult and beautiful journey of special needs, all while pointing the reader to Christ. Everyone needs a copy of *Real Families, Real Needs* on their bookshelf.

GILLIAN MARCHENKO

Author of *Still Life: A Memoir of Living Fully with Depression* and *Sun Shine Down*

The words were blurry . . . due to my tears . . . but the messages and testimonies are clear. Thank you to the many contributors here who allow us to humbly walk a bit with them on this sacred journey.

TOM VanWINGERDEN
Executive director, Friendship Ministries

Countless hurting people have been helped by the ministry of Joni and Friends over the years, and their new book, *Real Families, Real Needs*, is no exception to the quality of comfort they offer. As a psychologist, I know all too well the nature of the emotional suffering experienced by families with disabilities; and having grown up in one myself, I know these needs from the inside out. The courageous and thoughtful approach to addressing the needs of fathers, mothers, siblings, grandparents, and family members is both spiritually and psychologically sound. I could refer my clients to this book with complete confidence that they will find emotional help, and I plan to for many years to come.

MARK W. BAKER, PhD
Executive director of La Vie Counseling Center and author of *Jesus, The Greatest Therapist Who Ever Lived*

This book is helpful at many levels. In each of these chapters, there are stories of real people who are facing tough circumstances in families affected by disabilities. Through these stories, it becomes clear that God, the Creator of the Universe, loves each of us regardless of performance, abilities, or perceived holiness. God accepts us—not because of our worth or goodness but because of His love and goodness. In the midst of lives and families affected by disabilities, Jesus is making Himself known in amazing and personal ways, bringing great comfort. In the midst of life-changing diagnoses, we can choose fear and focus on our shattered dreams and numerous unknowns, or we can choose to trust God and believe that He is in control of every unknown. This book offers hope and many practical suggestions for moving in a positive direction toward life with Christ. I hope as you read it you will find help and hope in your journey.

PAMELA A. HARMON
Vice president, Young Life Capernaum

In February of 1998, the Ware family entered a world that we had heard, prayed, and read about but were personally detached from. When our son became a quadriplegic through an accident during basketball practice, our entire family was changed forever! We found ourselves facing multiple issues (e.g., emotional, financial, medical, spiritual, and living space) for which we were not prepared. We became intimately associated with a cultural group—families with disabilities, whom we had previously known only from a distance. Resources from a Christian perspective are needed for the encouragement and education of families with disabilities and those who live and serve with them. Joni and Friends has been providing encouragement and enlightenment to families with disabilities and those who serve with them for decades. *Real Families, Real Needs* is a timely, practical, and encouraging resource!

DR. A. CHARLES WARE
President, Crossroads Bible College

As a father who has faced tragedy in my family, I find *Real Families, Real Needs* to be authentic, practical, solid, biblical, and gritty. From the first page, tears welled up in my eyes as I read story after story from men and women facing what I've faced. If you are walking through that valley, you will want to take this book with you.

DAVID LYONS
International vice president of The Navigators Worldwide and author of
Don't Waste the Pain: Learning to Grow through Suffering

A Compassionate Guide
for Families Living with Disability

Real Families, Real Needs

Joni and Friends

FOREWORD BY *JONI EARECKSON TADA*

TYNDALE HOUSE PUBLISHERS, INC.
CAROL STREAM, ILLINOIS

FOCUS ON THE FAMILY

A Focus on the Family book published by Tyndale House Publishers, Inc., Carol Stream, Illinois 60188

Focus on the Family and the accompanying logo and design are federally registered trademarks of Focus on the Family, 8605 Explorer Drive, Colorado Springs, CO 80920. *TYNDALE* and Tyndale's quill logo are registered trademarks of Tyndale House Publishers, Inc. *Beyond Suffering* is a registered trademark of Joni and Friends. *EpiPen* is a registered trademark of Mylan Inc.

Unless otherwise indicated, all Scripture quotations are taken from the *Holy Bible*, New Living Translation, copyright © 1966, 2004, 2015 by Tyndale House Foundation. Used by permission of Tyndale House Publishers, Inc., Carol Stream, Illinois 60188. All rights reserved. Scripture quotations marked (NASB) are taken from the *New American Standard Bible.*® Copyright © 1960, 1962, 1963, 1968, 1971, 1972, 1973, 1975, 1977, 1995 by The Lockman Foundation. Used by permission. (www.Lockman.org). Scripture quotations marked (NIV) are taken from the Holy Bible, *New International Version*,® NIV.® Copyright © 1973, 1978, 1984, 2011 by Biblica, Inc.® Used by permission of Zondervan. All rights reserved worldwide. (*www.zondervan.com*) The "NIV" and "New International Version" are trademarks registered in the United States Patent and Trademark Office by Biblica, Inc.®

People's names and certain details of their stories have been changed to protect the privacy of the individuals involved. However, the facts of what happened and the underlying principles have been conveyed as accurately as possible.

The use of material from or references to various websites does not imply endorsement of those sites in their entirety. Availability of websites and pages is subject to change without notice.

Senior Editor: Pat Verbal, MA • Associate Editors: Chonda Ralston, MA, and D. Christopher Ralston, PhD • Assistant Editor: Rebecca Olson • Contributors: Deborah Abbs, Anna Brady, Cavin Harper, Rebecca Olson, Chonda Ralston, D. Christopher Ralston, and Pat Verbal

Cover and interior design by Beth Sparkman. Cover photograph of wall and pictures copyright © Tana Teel/Stocksy.com. All rights reserved. Cover photograph of stacked hands copyright © Raymond Forbes LLC/Stocksy.com. All rights reserved. Cover photograph of boy and girl on road copyright © duaneellison/Getty Images. All rights reserved. Cover photograph of boy on bicycle copyright © Jaren Wicklund/Adobe Stock. All rights reserved. Interior illustration of tree copyright © Klara Viskova/Shutterstock. All rights reserved. All other cover and interior photographs copyright © Joni and Friends. All rights reserved. Puzzle art of Joni Eareckson Tada on page ix by James Sewell. Used with permission.

Acknowledgments: William Denzel, The Denzel Agency, www.denzel.org

Joni and Friends International Disability Center
P.O. Box 3333, Agoura Hills, California 91376-3333
E-mail: cid@joniandfriends.org
Phone: 818-707-5664
Online: www.joniandfriends.org

For information about special discounts for bulk purchases, please contact Tyndale House Publishers at csresponse@tyndale.com, or call 1-800-323-9400.

Library of Congress Cataloging-in-Publication Data can be found at www.loc.gov.

ISBN 978-1-58997-925-3

Printed in the United States of America

23 22 21 20 19 18 17
7   6   5   4   3   2   1

Contents

Foreword

WHEN I BROKE MY NECK in a diving accident and suddenly became a quadriplegic, I felt as though God had walked into the room and upset the puzzle table. Not that I had everything figured out; it's just that before my accident, I figured my future would be a simple process of putting the puzzle pieces of my life together, all nice and orderly. I was looking forward to seeing my life picture easily fall into shape.

It's what most of us wish for our lives. But when your husband barely survives a debilitating stroke, or your elderly parent sinks into dementia, or your daughter breaks her back in gymnastics tryouts, or your baby is born with a genetic disorder you can't even pronounce, you feel as though God has thrown your family's puzzle against the wall.

You frantically scramble to locate the missing pieces, quickly solve the problem, and get your family back on track. But over time, you realize some key puzzle pieces are lost, and others simply don't fit anymore.

We hate it when life isn't fair! We expect our families to have the good life, with long stretches of ease and comfort and only occasional interruptions or irritations—frustrating, but easily bearable. Nothing bursts that bubble more quickly than a disability. A serious disabling condition is always a life changer for individuals and their families. Whether through stroke, a diagnosis of muscular dystrophy, or the loss of a bright and happy mind, we're suddenly awakened to the fact that life will never be the same.

It reminds me of my friend Susan who, when she learned that the child she was carrying had multiple disabilities, collapsed into her husband's arms and sobbed, "Our lives will never be the same! Never!" Brad held Susan tight, stroking and kissing her hair. Then he whispered, "Sweetheart, maybe our lives aren't supposed to be the same. Maybe God wants it that way."

Those were wise words. God has wired life to be difficult. Inconvenient and unwanted upheavals to our plans are part of what it means to live in a broken world. It's a jolt to find that life is not the bed of roses you or I anticipated. But it's necessary. And personal growth means learning how to deal morally and compassionately with these interruptions. Change potentially stretches the soul.

But here's the challenge: A disability can either bless a family or rip it apart. The choice often lies with us and the way we approach a family member with a chronic condition.

Will we remain hands off, or will we dare to roll up our sleeves and get involved? Will we play the blame game, or will we love full throttle? It's why the message in *Real Families, Real Needs* is so important. Whether you are a parent, grandparent, sibling, or other relative, this book will help you understand how a life-altering disability can and should draw your family closer to God and to each other.

God has placed disability in your family's midst so that everyone's life might be touched and changed. Disability has a way of pressing everyone up against each other—it's uncomfortable but necessary. Families would not have such significance if they did not, in fact, give us claim upon each other. And often it's the disability which creates the moral community that deserves to be called a family.

So, put the puzzle pieces away and fold up the puzzle table. God wants you to move beyond your urge to figure everything out and understand "how it all fits." Lean hard into His grace, and thank Him for the book you hold in your hands. Absorb the insights and life experiences of the fellow sojourners you'll meet in these pages. Put the principles to the test in your own family. And you'll find that change isn't as scary as you thought.

Two final words. First, you can trust the authors and contributors. Pat Verbal is a seasoned caregiver who spent the past ten years caring for her precious husband with Alzheimer's disease and her elderly mother. Both went home to heaven in 2017. Steve Bundy is the father of a teenage son with autism and physical disabilities. Neither Steve nor Pat are "textbook technicians"; rather, they are caring and compassionate family members who are intimately acquainted with the nonstop, 24/7 routines of never-ending disabilities.

Second, I'd like to extend a special thanks to our friends at

Focus on the Family who, like Joni and Friends, are dedicated to helping your family through prayers, resources, and practical support. It is my prayer that this remarkable book will be passed around to sisters, brothers, grandparents, spouses, aunts, and uncles. May every member of your family, young and old alike, be blessed, inspired, and motivated to welcome the change that God has brought into your midst through a disability. Yes, you can welcome that change . . . it's what family love is all about.

Joni Eareckson Tada
Joni and Friends International Disability Center

PART 1

A Father's Courage

1

Courage under Pressure

*Our family loved sports, especially cheering for our son Matt's
basketball team. It was all guts and glory until the day Matt made
a life-altering dive for a loose ball and broke his neck. But from
that first day, we clearly saw the hand of God at work. As Sharon
wept beside our son's body strapped to the hospital stretcher, Matt
looked into his mother's eyes and said, "Mom, pull yourself together.
Remember, God is in control!"*

*We prayed for healing, but God chose to show His glory through
human weakness. Withholding one miracle became an opportunity
for performing many miracles! Today Matt is a quadriplegic, but he
navigates his power wheelchair, drives his adapted van, plays video
games, and has never suffered from depression.*

*I'm so proud of my son. If our goal as believers is to communicate
the gospel message of faith, I must admit we have done a far better
job with a quadriplegic son than we did when he walked. Matt is
walking tall by faith, and God is walking with our family.*

DR. A. CHARLES WARE—
FATHER OF MATT AND BIBLE COLLEGE PRESIDENT

❧

HAVE YOU EVER RECEIVED a phone call that rocked your world?
Michael Hoggatt and his wife, Mandy, have. Their
daughter Summer, who has intellectual and developmental

disabilities, started bleeding a few days after her fifth birthday. After she underwent three months of testing, ultrasounds, and hospital visits, Michael and Mandy received a shocking call. The doctor told them to bring Summer to the hospital immediately, where a bed was waiting for her on the oncology floor. Following another series of tests, a surgeon confirmed that Summer had stage IV cancer. One of her kidneys would have to be removed the next morning or the cancer could prove fatal. Two years later—after undergoing life-threatening surgery, chemotherapy, radiation, CT scans, blood tests, IVs, and more surgery—Summer was cancer-free. She's a daily reminder of God's good gift of life!

Dr. A. Charles Ware also received a world-shaking phone call. He was away from his family on a speaking engagement when he was told that his athlete son, Matt, had been injured. "Your son has suffered a C4 fracture," said the calm, compassionate voice on the phone. "This means he broke his neck." Charles's wife, Sharon, called moments later with news that Matt was being transferred to another hospital, and she would be going with him. After Charles hung up, a rush of emotion rose within him. His legs barely held him up as he fought back the weakness and confusion of being so far from his family when they needed him.

Maybe you can relate to these men's stories—the shock, the uncertainty, the fear. If so, you're not alone.

Few things shake a man to the core of his being like hearing that his son or daughter has been diagnosed with a disability or severe illness. Some men receive this news in a delivery room or doctor's office, others in the chaos of an emergency room. Still others hear words such as "your child is not typical" during a parent-teacher conference at school and walk back to the car in shock, clutching pamphlets on special education services.

No matter where it's received, such news hits hard. Even men of strong conviction and integrity can easily lose their way and become plagued by anger, fear, and depression. These fathers may question what they thought to be true about life. And men of faith may wonder how a loving God could allow such a circumstance into their lives.

In the face of these realities, special-needs dads require a special kind of courage, which comes from knowing they are not alone. Many men have been raising children with disabilities for some time; they can show you how to climb the steep path ahead. These "travel guides" are able to point out where the loose rocks wait and help struggling fathers tie another knot at the end of their frayed rope. Even more important, God is climbing alongside you, continually working His good purposes amid seemingly impossible challenges.

Tempered Steel, Strengthened Lives

When hardships enter our lives, we can be sure that while *we* may be surprised by these things, God is not. He is always preparing us for challenges along the way. Like steel that has been subjected to intense heat until it becomes hard enough to sustain a tremendous amount of pressure and tension, so He has been tempering our spirits to be able to withstand the trials we now face.

Raising a child with a disability can be stressful on an average day. Then there are days when nothing works right, and we're bent under the weight of the situation. On those days in particular, we need to know that God is the Master Operator of our lives. He knows the right degree of heat required to temper our spirits, preparing us to be able to handle the pressure. God wants to lovingly mold us through life's high-temperature demands.

Are you leaning on God as your Father when pressures rise? If so, you'll experience the joy and peace of relying on Him and find yourself able to stand up under the weight of the struggle. As the writer of Hebrews puts it, "No discipline is enjoyable while it is happening—it's painful! But afterward there will be a peaceful harvest of right living for those who are trained in this way" (12:11).

Softened Hearts, Strengthened Spirits

When we face challenging times, it's easy to think, *This just isn't fair!* We too easily buy into the lie that Christians shouldn't have to go through hurtful struggles. If God is really in control, we would escape pain and suffering, right? No, God wants to teach us that difficult times can also be good. It is through pain and suffering that we can truly come to know Christ.

Paul reminds us that knowing God must be our highest priority. In Philippians 3:10-11 he says, "I want to know Christ and experience the mighty power that raised him from the dead. I want to suffer with him, sharing in his death, so that one way or another I will experience the resurrection from the dead!"

Such a declaration can only be made by a man of courage—one who has been tempered by life's hot spots and shaped under the gentle hand of a Father who watched His own Son suffer. Courage to share in our children's sufferings is not natural—it is a gift from God. It comes from walking closely with *Jehovah-Rapha*, the God who gives comfort in pain and sickness—who "heals the brokenhearted and bandages their wounds" (Psalm 147:3).

Whatever the specifics of your journey, you can be assured that God wants to build your character and strengthen your spirit through your role as a parent. His purpose is to soften your heart toward your family, your friends, and everyone you meet along the way.

God uses our children, with or without disabilities, to break down our hard attitudes and transform us into men of love and compassion. He uses the emotional (and sometimes physical) suffering that we experience to conform us into the image of His Son, Jesus Christ.

Why Me? Why *Not* Me?

Most would agree that hard times in moderate doses can be a good tonic for the soul. However, the suffering of our precious children is a different story! That kind of stuff can make strong men weak in the knees. Believers and nonbelievers alike are ready to cry out to God for mercy when their child's welfare is in danger. And when help doesn't arrive, we want to know why. The key is hidden in the questions we ask when we suffer.

"Why do I have to go through this?"

"Will I ever be happy again?"

"How can this possibly work together for good?"

The questions are focused on ourselves, not on God's plan.

After more than forty-five years as a quadriplegic, author and speaker Joni Eareckson Tada believes that suffering has a way of deflating self:

*Suffering is an important part of Christian living that
we all should know more about. Just keep the heat*

down to a manageable level, we think. We come
unglued, however, if suffering has us at the end of
our rope. But that's not a bad place to be. At that
point we are forced to think about a greater suffering
and turn to Christ on the cross. Don't ponder "me"
if you're hurting today . . . ponder the Messiah.[1]

Easier said than done! When you've just heard distressing
news from your child's doctor, teacher, or counselor, your
thoughts don't automatically jump to verses like "Do not be
anxious about anything" (Philippians 4:6, NIV). So how do
we adjust our focus off of ourselves and onto our Lord?

Adjusting Your Focus

Steve Bundy shares a pivotal "pondering the Messiah"
moment that transformed his life and profoundly altered his
relationship with his son, Caleb.

One night, Steve was emotionally and physically spent.
He was tired of asking God questions about his son's developmental disabilities and getting no answers. At that time, he
couldn't yet accept Caleb for who he was—he needed him to
be healed. Steve experienced grief and depression over Caleb's
condition and felt that his prayers fell silent at heaven's doors.
God seemed impotent as his world crumbled. He labored to
interpret Scripture out of his experience instead of allowing
Scripture to interpret his real-life experience.

At the time, Steve's church support group included friends
who believed that healing was for all—no exceptions! So
sickness, disabilities, and ailments all resulted from a lack of
faith. This group constantly prayed that Steve's faith would
increase, his sins would be confessed, and Caleb would be

healed. When he was not healed, they concluded that God's favor didn't rest on Steve or his family.

Steve later discovered that this false teaching focused on man's efforts and was based solely on one's perfection of faith rather than on the Word of God. But in his confusion, he was in a dangerous downward spiral and needed a new, God-centered perspective. One night that perspective broke in on him in a way he could not have predicted.

Many children with special needs have irregular sleeping patterns, and Caleb was no exception. One night when Caleb was two, he awoke crying, and Steve went to his room as usual to comfort him until he went back to sleep. As Caleb dozed off, Steve lay down on the floor and asked God why he had not *fixed* Caleb.

All the therapies and the doctors' visits, all the special time and attention aren't going to help Caleb's development, Steve told the Lord. *They won't fix him! Think of all the glory You would receive, Lord. The testimony of his miraculous healing would reveal Your glory to so many!*

What happened next shook Steve to the core. He shares his story:

> I am not one who would claim to have had many burning-bush experiences with the Lord. But at that moment, I sensed the presence of God filling Caleb's room so strongly that I cannot fully explain it in words. While I did not hear an audible voice, as clearly as I have ever heard anything, I heard these words flooding my soul: *Son, aren't you glad that I didn't require you to be fixed before I accepted you?*
>
> I couldn't move. I couldn't speak. I could only reflect on the words that pierced my heart and mind.

In a watershed moment that I can only describe as a revelation, an understanding of the unconditional love of my heavenly Father burst into my soul.

There I was praying for Caleb's brokenness to be fixed, and instead, I came to grips with *my own brokenness*. Suddenly it became clear to me that God, the, the Incarnate Word made flesh, the Spirit who moves within man, loved *me* unreservedly, regardless of my own performance, abilities, or perceived holiness. God accepted me not because of my worth or goodness. It is because of *His* love and goodness that I can cry out with confidence, "Abba, Father . . . Daddy!"[2]

In the same way, what flooded my soul that night was how utterly selfish, earthly, and unloving I had been to my own son, upon whom I had placed such high requirements.

> Dad, aren't you glad that God didn't require you to be fixed before He accepted you?

With tears running down my cheeks, I held my sleeping son in my arms and said, "Caleb, I love you just the way you are, for who you are, and I don't need you to be fixed. You are my son, and I'll love you unconditionally from this day forth, whether or not you are ever healed."

That moment changed my life. Despite my failures, I have been able to accept my son and rely upon God to form me into the father I'd always hoped to be. That night, for the first time, I realized that it wasn't Caleb who needed to be healed—it was me.

Now, many years later, Steve is amazed that he was blind to God's gift of his son. To be sure, Steve can't ignore the real disappointments and challenges that daily accompany life with disability. His family has experienced a great deal of discomfort and suffering throughout this journey, and as Caleb is becoming a teenager, the challenges continue to increase. As much as Steve loves his son for *who* he is, he does not always love the *way* he is. At the same time, Steve says, Caleb "is amazing and continues to be my greatest teacher. Without a spoken word, Caleb touches more hearts for Christ than a lot of Christians I've known."[3]

The Truth about Healing

Even if we recognize that God can use pain and suffering to soften our hearts, strengthen our spirits, and adjust our focus, when it comes to our children we still long for them to be healed—to not have to experience the challenges of life with a disability.

Like many believers, we can fall into the trap of focusing our attention exclusively on *physical* healing. Often, we can't comprehend how God might be glorified when a person is not healed physically. But the miracle of healing is that it is first and foremost *spiritual* in nature.[4]

The New Testament uses several Greek words for both physical and spiritual healing: *sozo, hugies, iaomai,* and *therapeuo.* For example, when Jesus spoke to the woman with the issue of blood, he said, "Daughter, take courage; your faith has made you well [*sozo*]" (Matthew 9:22, NASB). In the next chapter, Jesus commissioned the twelve disciples for ministry and gave them the mandate to "heal [*therapeuo*] the sick" (10:8). These examples are instances of physical healing, where a condition is completely cured.

But healing is also for the soul, as we find in Ephesians 2:8 (NASB): "By grace you have been saved [*sozo*]." Spiritual healing includes a right relationship with God. When a cure was the means to accomplish this restoration, Jesus did so. Otherwise, his ministry was to the heart and soul of mankind.[5]

It is natural to become disillusioned and tempted to abandon all hope when your family is affected by the evil of pain and suffering. Even though we may never fully understand the complexity of God's natural order, man is capable of experiencing God's goodness in the direst of circumstances. It is part of the mystery of the Christian faith—a mystery as old as Creation and as fresh as an alert on your smartphone.

Recognizing the Real Enemy

Satan employs an arsenal of weapons to attempt to discourage, defeat, and destroy. Fathers of kids and adult children with cerebral palsy, muscular dystrophy, spina bifida, and brain and spinal cord injuries must keep a vigilant watch to recognize the true enemy. The enemy is not the medical profession, not a bunch of random DNA cells, not the driver who caused the crash, and definitely not *you*! The enemy is Satan!

Some men fail to see this and live defeated lives. Others eventually come to accept this truth and learn to cope with the thousands of details of raising a child with a disability.

It helps to realize that Satan's abilities are also limited. That's right! Our enemy has disabilities! He is not free to do whatever he wishes. If he were, the world would be in far worse shape than it is now. God controls evil because He is good.

It took some difficult years of living with paralysis for Joni Eareckson Tada to put the topic of evil in its proper place in her life. "Evil can raise its ugly head only when

God deliberately backs away for a specific and intentional reason—a reason that is wise and good, even if hidden from this present life," Joni says. "God permits what He hates in order to achieve what He loves—it's just that most of us won't see it until the other side of eternity."[6]

Your Story Isn't Finished

Fortunately, God sometimes affords us glimpses of eternity in this life. Along the way, He reminds us that He can bring good out of any situation—including yours. He sees every moment you put into the care of your child and family. He sees the private tears, feels the hidden pain, and hears the recurring questions. He sees the love, the compassion, and the service you and your family give to one another. Isn't it reassuring that these things "count" with God? Regardless of what you've had to sacrifice to care for your son or daughter with a disability, your ability to love God and people has not diminished a single bit. If anything, you're probably more aware of opportunities to serve others than you ever were before.

When God has you in the refining fire, it's natural to cry out and beg Him to turn down the heat. But remember what's on the other side of that experience: a deeper, richer, more compassionate heart—the heart of our heavenly Father abiding in us.

Traveling Tips for Dads

When the pressure comes on strong . . .

Don't Walk Away!

Real men don't walk away—physically, emotionally, or spiritually. Real men seek ways to come to grips with their roles and responsibilities as husbands and fathers, even when the journey is not what they expected. Real men learn to live with another kind of courage.

Action Step: I will decide on several ways to spend quality time with my family, and then follow through.

Don't Lose Your Focus!

Emotional and physical challenges that accompany disabilities can sometimes be traumatic for the whole family. When dealing with a stressful situation, some dads count to ten, but it also helps to stop and picture Jesus standing beside you. Remember, He is the One who took on human form and is able to relate to whatever pressures you might face.

Action Step: I will choose a Bible verse from this book's chapter, write it on a note card, and focus on its truth this week.

Don't Forget to Laugh!

Laughter is like a refreshing stream encountered while walking along life's dusty trail. It gives us a moment to rest and refocus on life's God-given treasures.

Action Step: I will look for humor in the everyday and share those moments with my family.

2

Courage to Surrender
Your Family to God

When we refuse to turn our burdens over to God completely and don't allow Him to be in charge, we dishonor Him. It's like telling Christ that His death was in vain. Even though He repeatedly promises in His Word to show us the way, giving God control of my life was one of the hardest things I've ever had to do.

Yet I had to do it—or I wouldn't have made it through. God knew the lessons I needed to learn. He knew how much I would resist, and He knew what it would take for me to yield responsibility to Him for my life, my son, my future—everything.

DOUG MAZZA—FATHER OF RYAN AND
PRESIDENT AND COO OF JONI AND FRIENDS

❦

PERHAPS ONE OF THE MOST DIFFICULT aspects of finding ourselves in the refining fire of suffering is feeling like we've lost control. It turns out, however, that this is precisely where God wants us—especially if it leads us to surrender ourselves to Him.

Surrender Is Not Defeat

Contrary to what we might think, surrendering our wills and lives to God's sovereign care is not equivalent to being defeated. To defeat is to destroy, nullify, frustrate, or beat; to surrender means "to yield to the power, control, or possession of another."[1] And as Jesus Himself tells us, surrender is at the heart of the Christian faith. In Matthew 16:24 (NASB), He said, "If anyone wishes to come after Me, he must deny himself, and take up his cross and follow Me."

Jesus vividly modeled the true picture of surrender, especially in His last days on earth. After three years of teaching and traveling with His disciples, confronting the Pharisees' hypocrisy, healing hurting people, and feeding hungry crowds, He found himself at the end of His earthly journey. He had, no doubt, witnessed the gruesome practice of crucifixion. And being fully human, He prayed with a true sense of desperation, hoping to avoid such an excruciating death. Yet His prayer was also one of submission: "My Father! If this cup cannot be taken away unless I drink it, your will be done" (Matthew 26:42).

Just twenty-four hours later He was hanging on a rugged cross between two criminals in unimaginable agony of body and soul. But listen carefully and you'll hear His clear announcement of victory—not defeat! John penned his final moments: "When Jesus had tasted [the drink], he said, 'It is finished!' Then he bowed his head and gave up his spirit" (John 19:30).

If the Son of God had to give control of His life to God, His Father, how foolish are we, as mere men, to think that we can control our own lives or deaths?

Trading Control for God's Grace

You've heard the old adage "Father knows best!" In this case, it's true. All the academic degrees on planet Earth won't prepare you to comprehend the unfathomable purposes of God the Father. Man's intellectual apparatus is pitifully ill equipped to argue with his Creator. Yet most of us try at one time or another.

Doug Mazza found himself in this sort of situation. His son Ryan was born with a rare chromosomal imperfection that had deformed his skull, pushed his eyes nearly out of their sockets, and disrupted his upper respiratory system. By his third birthday, Ryan had undergone ten brain and skull surgeries.

For quite some time, Doug attempted to deal with things himself—in his own strength. He finally accepted his human insufficiencies during one of his trips to the end of his proverbial rope. After Ryan's tenth surgery, he was not responding to treatment, and it appeared that his life was slipping away.

In the hospital, Doug tried to find a comfortable position in the chair at Ryan's bedside. That chair had become his primary residence, and Doug was exhausted. Ryan's heart monitor nearly drove Doug insane as the green digits indicated a heart rate in excess of 180 beats per minute. Ryan had yet to reach his third birthday and was fighting for his every breath.

Sitting in that chair, Doug concentrated for a moment on what it felt like to be hugged by Ryan. Despite his deformities, Ryan's brain had developed to its full size, and he had a normal intellect for his age. Somehow, through all of the suffering, surgeries, and seizures, this little boy had acquired a sweet personality.

In spite of his developmental delays, Ryan would race on his hands and knees to greet Doug when he came home. Ryan always stretched out his somewhat deformed jaw into the warmest, most grateful smile Doug had ever seen.

But that night in the hospital, those joyful moments seemed to be ending. The doctor's words from three days earlier kept ringing in Doug's ears. With a hint of tears in his eyes, the doctor had said, "There comes a time when medical science has done all it can do, and for Ryan I'm afraid that time is now. I don't see how he can live longer than two or three more days."

So there Doug sat with a few family members, living between the resignation of impending loss and the hope of a miracle. He was keenly aware that his pleadings with God sat on a thin spiritual résumé.

He believed in God. He even believed that Jesus Christ was the Son of God. He just didn't know what that had to do with him. Certainly, he didn't have a personal relationship with Jesus. He believed that God surrounded the world and did with each day whatever it was He mystically decided. Like many people, there were times when Doug called on God—especially when he was in a tough spot—so he could ask something of Him or, maybe stated more precisely, try to negotiate with Him. And God seemed reasonable to Doug, Someone who was usually willing to do things his way. That's just the kind of God many of us want—One who will do our will! As Doug explains it,

> I was a guy who had to be in control. But Ryan had completely thrown my life's compass off-kilter. Like every situation I encountered, I had put myself in charge of my son's recovery, which was turning out to be the biggest failure of my life. I had exhausted every effort and had no other place to turn with this enormous, painful problem. My pleading prayers were going unanswered, my ability to manage in disarray.
>
> What possible purpose could the life of this child have? I had been offered all the bumper sticker wisdom and pop-Christianity phrases from all manner of people who, frankly, just didn't know what to say. Up to that point, the only role I could

see us playing for good was that other people were grateful they weren't us!

Three days after my meeting with the doctor, Ryan was clearly struggling. I couldn't even imagine where his strength to keep up the fight was coming from. I was alone with him at about four o'clock that afternoon. He had been in a coma, completely unresponsive for close to twelve hours, when he began to stir.

I rose from my chair and leaned forward. He rolled his head toward me, struggled to open his eyes, and recognized me as our eyes met. His eyes penetrated me in a way that has never happened before or since—and I will never forget it. He reached for me with what strength he had left, but a soft cloth was wrapped around his wrist and pinned to the sheet, protecting the opening where medicine flowed into his little body.

A look came over his face, and I knew exactly what he was thinking: *Daddy, help me! Help me! You're the one who said I would be okay. You're the one I trust; I don't know any power above you.*

And my heart broke. It broke because in that moment I knew I had never actually had such authority, and now I had only moments to make things right. I moved close to my son's ear, and for the first time, I said to him, "Ryan, I can't help you anymore. Jesus Christ is going to take care of you now." With that Ryan slipped back into his deep sleep, and I slipped down onto my knees, clinging to the side of the bed, in a complete emotional collapse.

In retrospect, Doug recognizes that there were several reasons for that collapse. First, there was the obvious emotion of the moment. But there was another reason too. Have you ever carried something that was unbearably heavy as far as you could possibly go—maybe even farther than you thought you could—and then released it? If you have, then you know the collapse that follows.

He could feel the weight being lifted off his shoulders.

Doug had carried the full weight of being in charge of Ryan from the moment he was born. That day in the hospital, for the first time, he had unwittingly, in faith, released the most important thing in his life to the living Christ. He could feel the weight being lifted off his shoulders. That is a picture of God's grace in action.

Ryan pulled through that day, to the amazement of his doctors. Eventually, Doug was able to take his son home from the hospital. In spite of his profound disabilities, Ryan's life has continued to be an inspiration to many, including his father. "When I asked God to save Ryan, He saved me," Doug says. "When I asked God to show me the purpose for Ryan's life, He showed me the purpose for my own life." It all began when Doug invited God to carry his load.

Let Go!

God will not elbow His way into our lives. The one thing God will certainly allow you to be in control of is what you are going to do with His Son, Jesus Christ: Accept Him or reject Him? Invite Him in or send Him away? His grace requires no secret handshake or classroom time.

His grace is immediately available upon the surrender of your life to Him. He'll meet you where you are and do the heavy lifting for you. If you are willing to receive Him as your Lord, He will mentor you and relate to you in a deeply personal way.

Giving control to God just takes one step—and that step is called *faith*! Faith requires release. God does not want half of your problem or half of your prayer. Sometimes we hang on to our issues, fears, problems, and needs as though they were a favorite worn-out pair of shoes. If you give Jesus all of yourself, He delights in giving you all of Himself. He is saying, "Let go."

Shifting Priorities

When we let go and hand the controls to God, He helps us think as He does. In the long run, this helps us gain peace in the midst of difficult circumstances that arrive when we parent children with special needs.

Before the birth of his third child, Will Kantz hadn't experienced any major hiccups as a parent. He realized that there would be adjustments in moving from one-on-one to zone parenting, but he was not prepared for his son and the way God would use Willson to address his own self-centeredness. Cornered by fatherhood, Will felt the nudge of the Holy Spirit and had to examine the intensity of his reactions to Willson's destructive urges.

As a result of his autism, Willson lived in a world of sensory confusion. His ability to perceive through the five senses was severely compromised. Vision, hearing, taste, and touch were not always trustworthy—his senses were a neurological train wreck that presented the world as chaos. One effect of this sensory confusion was destructiveness. Will wondered if his son would ever move beyond the toddler stage, in which everything was explored by mouth.

Will was, to say the least, completely unprepared for this challenge. All he thought he knew about parenting went up in smoke, because severe autism rearranges most parenting priorities. He and his wife no longer insisted on polite language; they were hoping and begging for any language. They focused less on potty training and prayed that Willson would stop smearing feces on the bedroom walls. Repeatedly, antique heirlooms and other valuable pieces of furniture were gnawed, bitten, tasted, yanked, bent, thrown, and otherwise tested. As Will recalls, "along with my dreams of a son, it seemed as if my peaceful home and the possessions I'd worked hard to accrue were in a toilet stuck on perpetual flush."

Gradually, however, Will's perspective began to change. God showed him that his love of himself and his "toys" (material possessions) were strongholds that he needed to confront as the sin of idolatry. Will's toys and treasures were a hindrance to his walk with Christ, who calls us to devalue material things and see people as invaluable. Now, Will recognizes his son as the most valuable "possession" he has:

> My son is a gift . . . just like he is . . . especially like he is. As I have shifted my materialistic outlook to a simple appreciation for my son, I've slowly adopted Christ's priorities. His priorities can lead to Christian maturity and a solid peace—one that the world (and all the stuff it offers) cannot take away. I thank my son for this gift.

Formula for a Successful Life

If you have never received Christ as your personal Savior, ask Him into your life today. You were created by Him and for Him. He has a good plan for your life!

Our own brokenness, sin, and rebellion have distanced us from God. God is holy and cannot accept sin or evil behavior. Like a judge, He must punish sinful actions. But like a father, He loves us and forgives us. Because God loves us, He sent His Son, Jesus Christ, to pay for our sins by dying on the Cross.

The Bible tells us in John 3:16, "This is how God loved the world: He gave his one and only Son, so that everyone who believes in him will not perish but have eternal life." Because Jesus Himself was holy, He did not deserve to die. As a result, He came back to life three days after dying. When we accept Him as our Savior—the One who died in our place— He gives His Spirit to live in us. The same Spirit who raised Him from the dead gives life to our own dead spirits.

Inviting Jesus into your life is simple. Romans 10:9-10 says, "If you openly declare that Jesus is Lord and believe in your heart that God raised him from the dead, you will be saved. For it is by believing in your heart that you are made right with God, and it is by openly declaring your faith that you are saved." Scripture also says that if we confess our sins, then He will forgive our sins.[2]

Begin by saying this simple prayer:

Father, I thank You for loving me and sending Your
Son, Jesus Christ, to die for me. I do believe that
He is Lord and Savior, and that He is alive today.
Forgive me of my sins, all the wrong things I have
done. Come into my life and change me. I will live

for You. I ask for Your help to be the man You want me to be. Amen.

Never, Never, Never Quit

Winston Churchill once said, "Never give in, never give in, never, never, never—in nothing, great or small." It's tempting to think that surrendering to God is tantamount to giving up. But *quitting* and *surrendering to God* are two very different things. The time may well come when you just want to quit and leave disability behind to start fresh on a different plan for your life. *Don't do it!*

Instead, join God's Health Club plan. Accept Jesus, read your Bible, pray and talk with the Lord, and you'll be renewed physically, mentally, and spiritually. Commit to believing God's promises, which requires faith. To have faith, you need to surrender to God, and surrender provides strength. And strength will produce endurance! Aren't strength and endurance what you need each day?

God has shown us throughout history that He never intended for us to be in charge; that's His role. Failure and frustration come from our unwillingness to accept the roles we were created to fill. Surrendering to God by following Christ and trusting His leadership is the first step to realizing His purpose for your life and your family.

Traveling Tips for Dads

You surrender your family to God when you . . .

Stop Trying So Hard

Every night I say a prayer over Caleb. As I watch him sleeping, I remind myself that God's love and

grace are greater than I can ever imagine. I don't hold
the mysteries of Caleb's life. They are far beyond
my grasp. I can say no to unrealistic pressures and
become utterly dependent on God.

STEVE BUNDY—FATHER OF CALEB, A TEENAGER WITH
AUTISM AND DEVELOPMENTAL DISABILITIES

Action Step: I will set a daily reminder on my phone to
stop and thank God for His awesome care and provision for
my family.

Make Use of Waiting Rooms

I've come to see waiting rooms differently as I've
learned about meaningful waiting and discovering
new opportunities. In waiting rooms, I have
opportunity to commune with God and find peace
in His presence. I can fill the needs of others who
wait by listening and offering insights in casual
conversation. I have opportunity to take stock and
contemplate decisions.

Through the years, my waiting rooms have
become preludes to joy. Time passes between each
waiting room visit, and I see my child grow—this
child whose life the doctors said was not viable. He
makes me laugh and shake my head in wonder. Now,
the waiting room is a reminder of God's care.

BRENT OLSTAD—FATHER OF BRYCE, A YOUNG MAN WITH
SPINA BIFIDA

Action Step: Next time I find myself in a waiting room,
I will intentionally strike up a conversation with someone
else who is waiting too.

Embrace Your Weaknesses

My weakness drove me into myself, but ultimately to the end of myself and into the arms of our heavenly Father. While I did not turn away from God or lose my faith when our twin girls were diagnosed with a disability, I was preventing myself from fully experiencing the love of our Creator. Embracing my weakness has been a process of embracing life's mysteries with gratefulness and trust. I've finally moved to a place of acceptance where I can celebrate human weaknesses. Now I share my journey with other dads with a prayer that it will open their eyes to the peace God wants to give them in their own weaknesses.

JON EBERSOLE—FATHER OF TWIN DAUGHTERS WITH CEREBRAL PALSY

Action Step: I will identify one area of weakness in my life and ask God to show His strength through me (2 Corinthians 12:9-10).

3

Courage to Stand as Brothers

Loss of control paralyzed me, as it does most men. It's like a javelin to the heart of our male egos to have a child with disabilities, because there's nothing we can do about it. In those early days, doubt crowded my mind: What kind of man am I? How could such a weak offspring come from me?

Men who have children without special needs have a hard time understanding how difficult it can be to reconcile your manhood with the apparent weakness of the child before you.

When Caleb was born, I longed to hear the affirmation, "You did not *do anything* wrong!*" But those words did not come until much later.*

STEVE BUNDY—FATHER OF CALEB AND SENIOR
VICE PRESIDENT OF THE CHRISTIAN INSTITUTE
ON DISABILITY AT JONI AND FRIENDS

❧

THE MOVIE *ACT OF VALOR* is a story about US Navy SEALs and their military exploits around the world. The film revolves around a letter written from a Navy SEAL commander to the son of a fallen SEAL, telling the boy about his father's courage, commitment, and honor. The fallen SEAL, through an act of heroism, had given his life for his comrades by throwing himself on a grenade. The movie is filled with emotional highs and lows as it depicts the incredible bond that Navy SEALs have with every team member and their families. Scenes move from high-adrenaline, life-threatening, top-secret missions to families gathered on the beach enjoying a moment when everyone is safe and out of harm's way.

In one especially poignant scene, it's the night before the SEALs leave for a mission, and they're gathered with their families. As the commander addresses the SEALs, he reminds them of the importance of taking care of things at home.

"Everything back home needs to be in balance," he says. "I mean, if things aren't right with the family, things aren't right with the finances or something's off, it's gonna pull us all out of balance. If somebody's got an issue, bring it up—everybody's got each other's back."

These men know that they need each other; there are no lone rangers in war. They are a band of brothers.

That scene captures what happens when fathers of children with special needs connect. We, too, are like a band of brothers. We may not be in life-threatening situations every day as Navy SEALs are, but we often live in life-altering situations and feel as if ammunition were raining down on us.

This band-of-brothers camaraderie is experienced powerfully when special-needs fathers are together. It doesn't take much time for the walls to start coming down so needs can be made known and assurances granted. Comments such as "How can I help?" "What do you need?" and "I am here for you!" become the norm. In essence, men begin to know that other men have their backs. Though we might not like to admit it, men don't want to do this thing called fatherhood alone.

Logjams to Friendship

Even so, there are a few major obstacles or logjams that keep dads from joining this band of brothers.

Isolation

When fathers of children with special needs were asked to identify their number one struggle, the common answer was isolation.

"They feel like they're the only person in the world going through this, which is so irrational," says Greg Schell, former director of the Washington State Fathers Network and the dad of a daughter with Down syndrome. "Thousands of people are born with disabilities every year, and they all have a dad."[1]

Schell believes the problem is that men become socialized differently than women, which often leaves men less prepared to handle a son's or daughter's disability.[2]

Poor Communication

Another logjam to building strong, solid friendships can be our lack of communication skills. This tactic of the enemy works to isolate us from our wives and children as well as from male friends. And it exposes our lives to even greater attacks, such as addictions, abuse, depression, and hopelessness.

There is a good reason why Peter describes the enemy as a lion: "Watch out for your great enemy, the devil. He prowls around like a roaring lion, looking for someone to devour" (1 Peter 5:8). A lion's natural instinct is to disperse a herd of goats or sheep so that one becomes separated from the rest and vulnerable to attack. The result is certain death for the animal and a warm dinner for the lion!

Thankfully, Scripture doesn't leave us without hope like unprotected sheep. Peter reminds us that there is strength in the brotherhood: "Stand firm against him, and be strong in your faith. Remember that your family of believers all over the world is going through the same kind of suffering you are" (1 Peter 5:9). He continues in that chapter to speak of friends who have supported him in times of need, such as Silas, a faithful brother, as well as those in the church at Babylon and his son in the Lord, Mark.

Denial and Withdrawal

A man's natural reaction to feelings of isolation and vulnerability can prompt him to further withdraw from others. We rationalize like this: *Don't talk about the issues, and perhaps they'll go away.* These thoughts lead us to pull back into a self-centered mode of handling life on our own. The problem is that this doesn't work very well—nor does it bring glory to God.

Busting up life's logjams requires the help of friends and brothers. As the apostle Paul prayed in Romans 15:5-6, "May God, who gives this patience and encouragement, help you live in complete harmony with each other, as is fitting for followers of Christ Jesus. Then all of you can join together with one voice, giving praise and glory to God, the Father of our Lord Jesus Christ."

Our bonds of friendship can glorify God, especially when we support each other in times of need. This was the case with Dr. Jeff McNair and Steve Bundy.

Jeff and his wife, Kathi, have not only given of themselves to spend time with Caleb when Steve and his wife, Melissa, needed a break, but Jeff has also come alongside them as an advocate for Caleb.

One of the many roles of fathers is to advocate for their children. If your child is school age, you are undoubtedly familiar with the Individualized Education Program (IEP) process (or at least you *should* be, so you don't put all the pressure of it on your wife!). Despite the many positive aspects of the special education system in the United States, parents still need to play an active role in the IEP process. We need to make sure that the "experts" are not making decisions for our children in a vacuum.

On one occasion, Steve and Melissa were having a difficult time with the IEP team. Despite how obvious it was to them that their nonverbal son needed an improved communication system, the IEP team was resistant to making an investment in new software or staff training. Jeff, who happens to be a professor of special education, attended the IEP meeting and intervened on behalf of Caleb and his parents. This was a major time commitment on Jeff's part. The meetings were spread out over three weeks and totaled more than twenty-four hours of time, but Jeff cleared his schedule to be there. In the end, Caleb received the communication system, and the staff received the training they needed to implement it.

Forming a Beachhead

There are all kinds of brotherhoods: sports teammates, golf buddies, business colleagues, charity supporters, neighborhood friends, mission teams, accountability groups, etc. But where can fathers of children with disabilities find strength through loyal relationships with other fathers who understand their journey?

If you're new to the world of disabilities, there are men who can mentor you. If you're a veteran at the systems affecting your son or daughter, you can help other men through support groups, online networks, or one-on-one counseling.

David Lyons, an international vice president of The Navigators, learned a lot about the fellowship of suffering after his twelve-year-old son, Ian, was diagnosed with cancer. David felt the isolation that fathers of children with special needs experience as they watch a loved one in pain. In his book *Don't Waste the Pain*, David shares a letter he received from a friend:

> There is a fraternity of suffering people. It's not an official group, and we haven't posed for a photo yet, but we know each other when we meet. Not one of us applied for membership. Suddenly we found ourselves having been inducted into this order.[3]

During his son's struggle with a very rare cancer that kills 98 percent of its victims, David encountered both the receiving side as well as the giving side of 2 Corinthians 1:4-5: "[God] comforts us in all our troubles so that we can comfort others. When they are troubled, we will be able to give them the same comfort God has given us. For the more we suffer for Christ, the more God will shower us with his comfort through Christ."

After Ian's funeral, David couldn't remember much of what people said, but he vividly recalls the comfort of a friend's hand on his shoulder and brothers who simply sat next to him in a silent show of support. In reflection he concluded,

> I don't know all of God's purposes for allowing pain into your life. But I know one: He intends to

comfort you so that you will comfort others. In fact, He intends the comfort you receive from Him to be so abundant that it can't help but overflow into the lives of others. Once you have entered into another person's pain, that comfort can take a lot of different practical forms—listening, talking, serving, or just showing up. But before we can comfort others in these ways, we have to get past the biggest obstacle the Devil puts in our way: self-centeredness.[4]

Have you ever noticed how discouragement, apathy, and sin come into our lives when we decide we can handle life on our own? No need for input from others—*I am my own man*, we think. The truth is that anything we can handle alone is temporary.

God has given us what we need for an abundant life and marriage, and we will not find it outside of time spent in Scripture, prayer, and fellowship. There is just no substitute. When we hide God's Word in our hearts as Scripture tells us to, we are less likely to sin against God and others.[5] When we come before God in prayer, He meets us at our points of need and gives us strength to meet the challenges at hand.[6] When we stay connected and accountable to brothers in Christ, we find courage to live out the Christian faith and be the men we desire to be.[7]

Building Bridges of Support

Have you ever visited the Golden Gate Bridge in San Francisco? It is truly an amazing sight! This engineering marvel boasts two main cables that span the bridge's 8,981 feet. There are 27,572 wires in each of those cables, with a total length that could stretch for 80,000 miles—more than three trips around the earth. The weight of the cables is 24,500 tons, which allows the bridge to carry a load of 4,000 pounds per foot—all hanging on two cables. And it has withstood numerous major earthquakes!

This is a perfect picture of the principle expressed in Ecclesiastes 4:9-10: "Two people are better off than one, for they can help each other succeed. If one person falls, the other can reach out and help. But someone who falls alone is in real trouble."

If you're part of a vibrant church community, you know the value of being connected with the larger family of God. All churches should be welcoming and empowering places where parents of children with special needs find friends and advocates ready to walk the difficult road ahead.

Sadly, this is not always the case. Many families have found repeated rejection or simply no outreach at all from the churches they've attended. As one man put it, "I hate to sound negative, but except in rare cases, a man stands alone with his special-needs situation."

From the beginning, God created the body of Christ to build ramparts against people's discouragement and depression. Christian men can become true brothers who work together in their journey to maturity by embracing life in a community of faith. When churches succeed, fathers of children with disabilities do not face life events alone. They are blessed to receive courage from the trustworthy example of others.

While we like to think of ourselves as self-sufficient islands, it's rare to find a father who regrets spending time with other dads. The reality is that we all need support. And when we support each other, bringing our unique gifts, skills, and perspectives into play, something wonderful takes shape: God begins to weave the threads of our individual lives and families into a larger tapestry, a masterpiece of which each of us is an indispensable part. As someone once said, God did not write solo parts for very many of us. He expects us to be participants in the great symphony of life.

Sometimes it doesn't take much for us to become brothers in Christ to one another. A phone call, a visit, or simply letting a father know we're available can make a world of difference to a lonely person. Are you a father who can reach out to another dad? Can you let a man know that you care about his family? Or maybe you are the man who needs to ask for help from another dad. Either way, you are not alone. Reach out.

Paying It Forward

Dave Deuel became part of a family group shortly after his daughter was born with Down syndrome. The seed to do so was planted by a doctor, who advised Dave and his wife to take Joanna home and treat her like their other kids. Then he told Dave about another couple who had given birth to a child with Down syndrome the same day Joanna was born and urged him to call this couple for mutual encouragement. Dave says,

> In one short but life-changing conversation, a wise and caring doctor had moved me from personal tragedy to personal mission. We couldn't wait to call the other couple, Jeff and Shirley. My wife and Shirley became close friends almost instantly. Jeff and I were stamped from the same mold—had no

siblings, grew up in small towns, and came from solid Christian homes. The compatibility seemed like a breath of fresh air. We were not alone. As we walked into their home for the first time, we were warmly welcomed. We started off by doting over our two little round-faced sweethearts, side-by-side in their carriers. The afternoon passed quickly with chicken on the grill, lots of laughing with a little crying, and plenty of advice exchanged. Toward the end of our time together, someone said, "Hey, we need to form a group for families with children with Down syndrome." Encouraged and blessed, I thought to myself, *[W]e already are a family group.*[8]

God works through family groups like Dave's to strengthen homes and open doors for male friendships that might otherwise be missed. It doesn't take much to get started. Just invite another father of a child with disabilities to lunch or ask him and his family over for dinner. You might be surprised how God can go before you to bridge the gap and to build new bonds of friendship.

The Washington State Fathers Network was created to help men "pay it forward" by sharing whatever life stage they are in with other fathers. The organization promotes fathers as "crucially important people in their children's and families' lives." "We firmly believe men are superb resources for each other and fathers have special needs of their own when it comes to raising a child with a chronic illness or developmental disability," reads a statement on its website.[9]

Dietrich Bonhoeffer—pastor, theologian, and WWII prisoner—loved his brothers and sisters in Christ. His love for them transcended affinity. He wrote in *Life Together*, "The

Christian, however, must bear the burden of a brother. He must suffer and endure the brother. It is only when he is a burden that another person is really a brother and not merely an object to be manipulated."[11]

Like those Navy SEALs who have committed their lives to one another, we have the privilege and responsibility to band together with other fathers. After all, just as those SEALs need to know they can depend on other men who have their backs, we need to know that we have brothers backing us up on this journey called fatherhood.

Benefits of One Fathers Group[10]

- Anxiety decreased 97 percent
- Feelings of joy increased 67 percent
- Family relationships improved 77 percent
- Having someone to talk to increased 80 percent
- Feelings of helplessness decreased 57 percent

Traveling Tips for Dads

In order to build a band of brothers . . .

Find Friends for the Journey

Let's be blunt: You won't make it alone. Strong friendships are crucial to navigate such a challenging road trip. By connecting with other men for lunch meetings or support groups, you can overcome discouragement, apathy, and even sin.

In his book *The Father Connection*, Josh McDowell says that fatherhood "may be the most frightening job in the world, but it is also the most important, most rewarding job any man can tackle."[12]

Action Step: I will invite another father to read Josh McDowell's book and discuss it with me.

Find Rest Stops along the Way

Joni and Friends Family Retreats provide the whole family with a refreshing and strengthening week at a Christian camp. Couples and single parents learn to trust and appreciate the short-term missionaries who are assigned to care for their children.

Action Step: I will look for the next Joni and Friends Family Retreat in my area and start a savings account so I can take my family. See www.joniandfriends.org/family-retreats.

Respite Programs such as Buddy Break by Nathaniel's Hope give parents a much-needed break and opportunities to connect with each other and other couples. Respite events may be offered weekly or bimonthly, for half or whole days. See www.nathanielshope.org.

Action Step: I will contact my local church to inquire about nearby respite program options.

Find Volunteer Opportunities

Special Olympics, The Miracle League, and many other groups bring dads together to raise awareness, provide funding, and just have *fun*! Dads know that nothing lifts the spirit like teamwork!

4

Courage to Trust in God's Eternal Plan

Even though my son Ryan has never spoken a word in his life, I'm confident that if he were to die today, he would go straight to heaven. Ryan has never recited the "sinner's prayer" and may not even understand the concepts of sin and repentance. But I believe that God's grace covers those with intellectual disabilities who are unable to grasp such abstract ideas. I also know that people with intellectual disabilities often understand much more than they seem to comprehend.

My son, who is now thirty-six years old, has never spoken a word to me, and the doctors say he has the intellect of a six-month-old child. Still, I have presented the entire gospel to him and asked him to receive Christ into his heart. I knew that as his father it was my responsibility, even though I had no way of knowing how much Ryan truly understood. It brought me great comfort as well. Did I need to take that step? Maybe not, but if I share the gospel with others, why would I not share it with my own son?

DOUG MAZZA

❦

In the previous three chapters, we explored the courage it takes to face the realities of pain and suffering, especially when it involves your own child. We emphasized the importance of surrendering control over your family to God and the necessity of having "brothers"—other fathers of children with disabilities who can walk this difficult road along with you.

Now we must face the most difficult topic of all: the possibility that you may outlive your child who has a disability. This is never a pleasant issue to consider, but for the sake of our families, it must be faced head-on.

Standing on the edge of despair can become almost commonplace for families with children who are medically fragile. Unfortunately, many people want to steer clear of us when we're in such a situation. They aren't necessarily being cold or uncaring; they simply don't know what to say, and avoidance is easier. Some well-meaning visitors try to share a Bible verse or cliché in an effort to cheer us up. But even while we know that the Bible is true and our friends' intentions are good, such sentiments can feel unkind—even cruel—in the moment.

We often return to the story of Job in the Bible because we relate to his grief as a father. You'll remember how his friends were seemingly well intentioned. They started out right by showing up to support their friend who had lost almost everything. But then they blew it by opening their mouths. They started preaching to Job and telling him all the reasons he was suffering, but they were so wrong. They truly had no idea what was happening. Job didn't hesitate to speak up and tell them, "If only you could be silent! That's the wisest thing you could do" (Job 13:5).

We See But a Glimpse

Job was grieving the loss of his children and struggling to comprehend why his world had been turned upside down. There were no easy answers—there never is when a child dies. In his book *Trusting God: Even When Life Hurts*, Jerry Bridges writes, "Adversity is difficult even when we know God is in control of our circumstances. In fact, that knowledge sometimes tends to aggravate the pain. 'If God is in control,' we ask, 'why did He allow this to happen?'"[1]

Bridges lost his mother at age fourteen and later watched his wife succumb to cancer. He wrote the book as a result of his own struggle to understand God's divine sovereignty in light of pain and suffering. Bridges goes on to provide an analogy showing that the journey of life is like walking along a path with a thick curtain just ahead, limiting our view of what awaits. "None of us can tell what is beyond that curtain; none of us can tell what events a single day or hour may bring into our lives."[2] Bridges then circles back to the issue of leaning into our faith and trusting in God's goodness through all life's unknowns—no easy task, especially in light of what we might be asked to face.

What's weighing on your mind today? What uncertainty do you need to bring before your heavenly Father?

Philippians 4:6-7 is a passage many of us have memorized: "Don't worry about anything; instead, pray about everything. Tell God what you need, and thank him for all he has done. Then you will experience God's peace, which exceeds anything we can understand. His peace will guard your hearts and minds as you live in Christ Jesus."

David Lyons discovered firsthand what this means. While Ian battled cancer, David learned to pray big prayers. As a leader, he had asked many times for divine wisdom. Now, as a parent, he craved supernatural wisdom more than ever. After all, it was his child's life at stake!

David found guidance in the words of James 1:2-5, which tells us to view trials as our friends and urges us to ask God for wisdom in the midst of them. Moreover, the passage assures us that God will give wisdom to those who ask for it—and He will give it without finding fault or rebuking us for asking!

Prayer Is Essential

At the very end, even when you're facing what seems to be the final battle, prayer is still essential. In a journal entry from that time and in his book *Don't Waste the Pain*, David expresses the ongoing importance of praying, even when the answers aren't what you desire:

> *We've been praying crazy faith prayers here. I feel like one of those pilots in a Star Wars movie, strapped in for a life-or-death firefight. I engaged in the spiritual battle in earnest Saturday afternoon. At 11 that night Renee texted me from home to say good night, and I replied that it would be awhile before my head would hit the pillow. I was still stoked and going after it in prayer. But soon the Lord impressed on me that He gives to His beloved even in his sleep. So I slept until about 6 a.m., then resumed my part in this battle, while Ian carries on his. . . .*
>
> I prayed fiercely. I prayed as I wanted others to pray for me. I prayed as we had prayed before, when we'd seen God do the miraculous again and again. But I was about to learn that praying is not always about getting the results we hope for. Sometimes God has something even bigger in mind.[3]

When Jesus Calls

We all know that parenting is only for a season, whether a child has a disability or not. But parents of a child with life-threatening disabilities are not releasing their precious daughter to her betrothed or delivering their son to a university. Many of them live each day with the thought that someday they'll likely stand before their child's casket.

In chapter 2, we saw how Doug Mazza learned to surrender his son to God. When Ryan was born, his prognosis was grim. Doctors said that he probably would not live past age three. His parents felt stuck in a day-to-day kind of existence, hesitant to look beyond the next twenty-four hours. As Ryan continued to defy the odds and outlive the doctors' predictions, Doug was able to embrace the fact that only God knew how many days they would enjoy with their son. Psalm 139:16 assured them that every day of their son's life had been written about before one day came to pass. God knew whether Ryan would reach his fourth—or his fortieth—birthday. He knows every detail of your child's life too.

Even so, it is gut-wrenchingly difficult to let go, as David Lyons found to be the case during his son's last days. One afternoon, David and his wife, Renee, had a profound time alone with their son, Ian, who was alert and seemed to be "with" them. Tears were flowing abundantly as David told his son "something like this":

> Ian, I'm sure that somehow in the midst of all this Jesus is making Himself known to you in amazing and personal ways. And we want you to know that however HE is leading you, we want you to follow HIM. As far as we can understand His leading, we believe that He intends to heal you. But if He is clearly telling you that He wants you to leave us and go home to be with Him, then we want you to do that. I really mean that. Even though in the coming

hours and days you'll hear us intensely battling for your healing in prayer, if Jesus Himself is calling you home, go for it. Don't worry about disappointing us. That would be very hard for us, but we'd be happy for you. However, if you hear Jesus calling you to fight, then I want you to FIGHT with all you have. I know this has been incredibly hard for you. But if Jesus is telling you to fight, then He will strengthen you. Don't lose heart, son. Just follow Jesus however He leads you. And He will enable you.[4]

Ian answered Jesus' call home the next day. David later sought solace in the book of Job. He found a man—much like himself—agonizing over the death of a child and struggling to comprehend the *why*.

Dr. Larry Waters, professor of Bible exposition at Dallas Theological Seminary, writes extensively on the book of Job. He says, "Life is more than a series of absurdities and unexplainable pains that one must simply endure, it is a life linked with the unseen purpose and destiny of God. . . . God does allow suffering, pain and even death, if it best serves his purpose and destiny for his creation."[5]

Best? How could the death of a child ever serve God's purpose?

God's Plan, Not Ours

If someone had asked Tim Kuck that question after the loss of his four-year-old son, he probably couldn't have fathomed an answer. Now in hindsight, Kuck sees the ripple effect from his son's life and death. But this valuable insight came to Tim only after a season of indescribable grief and depression.

Tim's son, Nathaniel Timothy Kuck, was born on June 6, 1997, and died November 13, 2001. His short life was never what Tim had dreamed of for his only son; as Proverbs 19:21 puts it, "You can make many plans, but the LORD's purpose will prevail."

Tim and his wife, Marie, welcomed Nathaniel home from the hospital when he was only eighty-nine days old and weighing four pounds. His nursery looked like an IC unit, with feeding tubes, IVs, and heart and oxygen monitors. At first they believed that Nathaniel had an unidentified syndrome since tests at Boston Children's Hospital had been inconclusive. Later, though his condition was never completely diagnosed, it exhibited similarities to craniosynostosis, with other complications, which is a disorder where the skull plates prematurely fuse together, prohibiting brain growth.

In spite of Nathaniel's seven major surgeries, Tim's daily life settled into a routine, with Marie serving as an excellent caregiver. But underneath his calm mask, stress was taking its toll on Tim.

When Nathaniel was about three, Tim found himself in an "emotional funk." His poor attitudes warned of a pending depression. Oddly enough, Tim had never had much grace for negative, pessimistic people. He had always wanted to tell them, "Get a life! Get off the couch, stop whining, and do something." But now *he* was the whiner!

By the grace of God and over time, Tim eventually pulled out of his serious depression. He and Marie determined to do everything possible for Nathaniel and to trust God with the impossible. Life returned to normal for a season. Although Tim rarely traveled because of Nathaniel's condition, in 2001 he accepted an invitation to speak at a missions conference in another state.

On November 10, 2001, Marie drove Tim to the airport along with their three children, including Nathaniel, who was four. At the curb, Tim opened the sliding door of the van and kissed his son on the head. Their "little man" was sick, but since he'd spent 150 days of his young life in hospitals, it wasn't unusual.

Tim spoke at churches the next two days. When he talked with Marie the first day, Nathaniel had become a little more congested and was getting breathing treatments. The following night, Marie told Tim she expected to spend the night with Nathaniel, sitting upright in an easy chair. At 6:00 a.m., Tim's phone rang. It was Marie, and she was frantic. She and Nathaniel were in an ambulance, and he was not breathing. She feared their son was dead. The paramedics were doing their best to resuscitate him, but to no avail. Without their consent, without their permission, their little boy had changed addresses—from earth to heaven. His body remained, but his spirit had left. Nathaniel had died of a cardiac arrest.

Gripped with grief and indescribable pain, Tim packed his bags and drove eighty miles to the nearest airport. As he sat in the terminal, emotionally distraught, he heard the throng of people surrounding him, talking on their cells or working on laptops. Others played with their kids, who were excited about going to Disney World. The whole scene seemed terribly wrong to Tim.

As he recalls, "I wanted to shout from the top of my lungs, 'Stop! Don't you know my son is dead?! It's not right for life to continue as normal. The whole world should pause in silent grief over the loss of this beautiful child.' Nothing stopped. Yet, *my world* had forever changed."

Putting one foot in front of the other, Tim and Marie stumbled through the details of burying their child. Dates and service plans were scheduled, yet the idea of burying one whom they loved so much was hard to digest. They decided that the funeral would be a celebration of Nathaniel's short life. Even though they were gripped with his absence, they committed to honor the God who took their son without permission or warning. God had appointed his life and knew him by name: *Nathaniel*, which means "treasured gift from God."

As the waves of grief began to subside, Tim and Marie thought back on their family times with a child who had special needs. They realized that from the time Nathaniel was born, people did not know what to do with their family, even people in the church. Families like theirs just did not fit into a mold.

People didn't ask them out to dinner or over to their houses. Babysitters were too intimidated to care for their son because of his health. Tim and Marie knew that some Christians wanted to do more but felt as if they were not equipped to help.

That is when the Kucks started a ministry called Nathaniel's Hope, which partners with local churches nationwide to develop respite programs called Buddy Break[6] and hosts an annual party in downtown Orlando to honor families that have kids with special needs. The festival, Make 'm Smile, is saturated with a spirit of joy and is held on Nathaniel's birthday. Attendance has grown from six hundred people in 2004 to approximately fifty thousand in 2016.

Isn't that just like God! A four-year-old boy who never walked, talked, or ate by mouth has shown thousands of people that every life has a God-appointed purpose. In hindsight, Tim now sees how God redeemed the loss of their son. Nathaniel's smile continues to shine the light of hope upon hurting families that need to know the love of God.

Estate Planning for Our Children

As difficult as it is to prepare for the potential loss of our children, we must consider the possibility that we might die before they do. One of the most serious worries on any father's heart is the question, What will happen to my child and my family if I'm no longer here to provide for them?

Much like wise leaders create succession plans for businesses, a caring father must consider his family's estate-planning needs. Often these matters seem too sad to talk about and are set aside with a promise to handle them later. Unfortunately, though, we're not promised ample notice of when we will be called home to be with Jesus.

There are a few practical steps that all parents should take to protect their children, especially if they have a son or daughter with a disability. Every family should establish a living trust with a selected conservator for the children. Hire an attorney to make it formal and legal. Otherwise, the government will take over and make critical decisions about your child's future—and no one will care as much as you do.

A special-needs trust is a legal document containing instructions directing the management and distribution of the resources placed in the trust. The person creating or funding the trust is the grantor. The person who receives the benefit or on whose behalf the trust was created is the beneficiary. The trust allows you to leave any amount of money to your child without jeopardizing government benefits.

Funds in a special-needs trust can make a big difference in quality of life by paying for things such as insurance, personal-care attendants, or rehabilitation. A number of good organizations are available to advise families in establishing a special-needs trust, such as the Special Needs Alliance.[7]

Whether choosing a family member or a friend, it is essential to consider a responsible person as your child's conservator. Make sure that he or she will genuinely care about your child when you're absent—don't choose someone who simply feels obligated. Conservators don't need to have a lot of money—what they need is a lot of heart. If you don't have someone in mind, begin praying for the Lord to bring the right person into your life.

Once you've selected a conservator, begin including that person in some family activities and specifically in strategic meetings regarding your child, such as his or her school Individualized Education Program (IEP). Invite the conservator along as an observer so that he or she will have a better idea of your child's abilities and reactions.

Discuss every aspect of your child's future, from finances to health care to living arrangements and the basics

Funds in a special-needs trust can make a big difference in quality of life.

of day-to-day life. Don't leave the important things up to chance or interpretation. Tell the conservator what you think and how you feel about your child's future. Involvement is the key to helping him or her understand how you approach decisions, and it will help to create a smooth transition if one becomes necessary.

No Easy Answers, Just Truth

In each of these chapters we've shared stories of real people who are facing tough circumstances in families affected by disabilities. Our prayer is that you have begun to see that God is big enough to handle whatever it is that you and your child encounter today and in the days ahead.

This is true courage—to get up each day and do the next right thing; to trust God's plan one day—maybe one hour—at a time.

Perhaps the best encouragement we can offer comes from what the Lord said to a man named Joshua. With these words, God encouraged Joshua to lead His chosen family, the Israelites: "Be strong and courageous. Do not be afraid; do not be discouraged, for the LORD your God will be with you wherever you go" (Joshua 1:9, NIV).

How is it possible for us to do this? Because the God of the Universe willingly sacrificed His own Son, we can rest in the assurance that He cares about our fears as well as our children's pain and suffering.

Take courage in God's eternal plan for you and your family, living each day in the hope of our Savior and coming King, Jesus Christ!

Traveling Tips for Dads

Trust God's eternal plan for your family.

Face Crossroads by Holding on to Hope

As Christians, we are asked to carry a vision—a "future-sight"—for those who die before us. This hope is so wonderful that it is indescribable: "'No human mind has conceived'—the things God has prepared for those who love him" (1 Corinthians 2:9, NIV).

In his book *Nearing Home,* Billy Graham says, "We were not meant for this world alone. We were meant for Heaven, our final home. Heaven is our destiny, and Heaven is our joyous hope."[8] This also applies to our children.

Action Step: I will search out Scripture passages about hope and heaven and pray for a greater vision of eternal things.

Consider Your Family's Estate Plans

It is understandable that some men tend to avoid end-of-life issues. However, most find that after decisions have been made and the paperwork finalized, it brings great comfort to the whole family. For help see www.findlaw.com and www.estate.findlaw.com /trusts/special-needs-trusts-faq-s.html.

Action Step: I will consider creating a special-needs trust to protect my family.

Share Your Grief—Share Your Hope

Romans 12:15 says, "Be happy with those who are happy, and weep with those who weep." Don't worry about finding the "perfect" or "right" words to say. The most important thing is simply to be available.

One day as Ryan battled in the ICU to survive, I experienced one of my lowest points. My friend Buck—a tough Vietnam War door gunner— somehow knew what to do. Without my asking, he showed up at the hospital and sat silently next to me. Eventually, we went in to see Ryan, who was in a coma following surgery, his bandaged head revealing only his eyes. As Buck stood there with me, he started weeping. I can't explain it, but that moment brought me great comfort. I felt the love and understanding of a true friend.

DOUG MAZZA

Action Step: I will put my hope into action by helping other hurting and grieving families in my church and community.

PART 2

A Mother's Heart

5

A Troubled Heart:
Embracing Your Child's Diagnosis

"We see all of the red flags for Down syndrome."

I'd been so eager to hear the results of my ultrasound, but the doctor's blunt announcement took my breath away. For the first time, I understood the panic and desperation I'd sensed while holding my young friend Brittany's hand at the crisis pregnancy center where I volunteered. I remembered reassuring her, and many other girls, that she could handle whatever obstacles she faced. I encouraged these moms to look beyond their circumstances and to keep their babies. But there I was, filled with panic and fear of the unknown. What the doctor said next hit me like a kick in my gut . . . "In a case like this, we recommend termination."

The stiff paper on the examination table made crinkling sounds beneath me. I think I groaned aloud as I prayed silently: Jesus, rescue me. Rescue my baby. This can't be happening. It can't be true. This stuff happens to other people, Lord. Not to us, God. Not to our little girl. Please, God.

SHAUNA AMICK—MOTHER OF SARAH

❦

LIFE IS FILLED WITH ORDINARY DAYS. But now and then there's a moment when something happens—and nothing is the same again. Whether the news comes from an ultrasound or is the result of a battery of tests, a mother is never prepared to hear that her child faces a disability or a life-changing diagnosis.

There is a profound sense of grief as reality sets in and a mother must accept the loss of the typical hopes and dreams that all parents have for their children. Kristin Reinsberg, a marriage and family therapist, says it's a feeling of significant loss akin to a death or divorce.

"Recent research has indicated that parents of children with special needs may even experience feelings and symptoms of traumatic stress, particularly at the time of their child's diagnosis," she says.

Reinsberg warns that the stress can be compounded when parents are hesitant to acknowledge or express their feelings of anger, depression, or fear because they want to appear strong or feel they need to be positive. "It is important for families to understand and talk about these feelings, and to know that what they are feeling is natural."[1]

Ellen Stumbo, a mother of a daughter with Down syndrome, knows this from experience. "Nothing, nothing compares to the thick net of overpowering emotions that capture you as you deal with your child's new diagnosis," she says.[2] Stumbo is a popular blogger who encourages mothers of children with special needs by sharing her own lessons learned along the way. She recalls wrestling with the fear of the unknown when her daughter was born. She had no idea how the diagnosis would impact their future: "What will her future look like? What about mine? Will she live with us forever? Will she ever have a job? And why me? *Why me!*"

These are tough questions, but they are the same questions most moms wrestle with, if they're willing to be honest. Mothering can be hard, and it's even harder if we're not willing to acknowledge our weaknesses and find others to come alongside us. Moms, God's desire is for us to minister to one another and help each other through life's hardships: "He comforts us in all our troubles so that we can comfort others. When they are troubled, we will be able to give them the same comfort God has given us" (2 Corinthians 1:4).

Stumbo's authenticity and transparency with her own struggles have drawn women to her work. While she concedes that circumstances feel overwhelming in the beginning, Stumbo offers assurances of hope that the sadness will eventually peel away layer by layer. "The lost dreams will be replaced by new dreams. . . . I've been where you are, and I can tell you the light will come, joy will show up, love will take over."

Philip Yancey has written a great deal about the struggle to trust God through times of pain and suffering. In his book *Where Is God When It Hurts?*, he writes, "A wise sufferer will not look inward, but outward. There is no more effective healer than a wounded healer, and in the process the wounded healer's own scars may fade away."[3]

A Fearful Heart

Tonya remembers praying for her baby as she endured two days of painful labor. When she finally held little Abby for the first time, all her miniscule fingers and toes were accounted for, and Tonya declared their child "perfect" as her husband leaned in for a kiss.

Their perfect life became a nightmare only two months later when Abby's small frame began to convulse, lurching to and fro, and her eyes rolled back in her head. Although the seizure lasted only a few minutes, it felt like hours as the couple rushed their daughter to the nearby children's hospital.

More seizures followed, increasing in both intensity and frequency. Medical staff quickly filled the emergency room, asking questions and examining Abby. Tonya could only watch as nurses carried her baby from one test to another. *What is happening? Why aren't they telling us anything?* Tonya found herself wringing her hands as her husband paced back and forth waiting for answers.

Abby was diagnosed with an unknown seizure disorder. The doctors said she would probably not live long, and her life would be filled with many challenges.

Do you recall that moment in time when it first hit you that things would never be the same again? Were you in an emergency room, a doctor's office, a school classroom? Were you trying to play with your sweet child, only to realize something wasn't quite right? Did you get a call from a teacher recommending testing? Did you walk into a room where your once vibrant child lay motionless on a stretcher?

We can either let fear grip our hearts or choose to trust God.

In times like these we face a choice: We can either let fear grip our hearts and convince us to focus on our shattered dreams and numerous unknowns, or we can choose to trust God and believe that He is in control of every unknown and loves our children even more than we do! "You have not received a spirit that makes you fearful slaves. Instead, you received God's Spirit when he adopted you as his own children. Now we call him, 'Abba, Father.' For his Spirit joins with our spirit to affirm that we are God's children" (Romans 8:15-16).

Fear wants to make you believe there will never be another sunny day or another reason to smile, and no one will ever relate to what you're feeling. Fear is a thief. Satan is the author of fear, and he wants to rob us of the joy God has planned for us—and for our children. "The thief's purpose is to steal and kill and destroy" (John 10:10).

God, on the other hand, is a giver—the Giver of life, courage, and better tomorrows. Jeremiah 29:11 promises plans for our good, for "a future and a hope." This can be hard to fathom or even seem trite when your child faces a life-altering diagnosis, but it doesn't make it less true. God is also the Giver of new eyes—of twists in perspective and rearranged priorities.

Have you ever come to a place of being grateful for something you originally thought might do you in? That's right, even grateful for disability or disease?

Christy saw God bring beauty from the ashes of disability and debilitating depression (Isaiah 61:3). Her daughter, Emily, was diagnosed with a rare disorder only six days after birth, which caused thinning of the arteries in her brain, resulting in strokes and seizures. As a missionary and a pastor's wife, Christy had always assumed her faith would remain strong through life's trials. But Christy had never considered the possibility of watching her newborn baby's body racked by seizures. Her whole world was shaken.

After Emily's diagnosis, Christy felt waves of grief that intensified with feelings of fear, anger, disbelief, and helplessness. Christy admits that she felt as if she were drowning in the tumultuous tsunami waves of her emotions. Many days she felt as if she could barely hold on. But with the help of friends and family, Christy began to refocus on the God who commands the wind and rain . . . and the waves. She read in the book of Mark where Jesus and some disciples found themselves in a boat during a terrible storm:

Soon a fierce storm came up. High waves were
breaking into the boat, and it began to fill with water.

Jesus was sleeping at the back of the boat with
his head on a cushion. The disciples woke him up,
shouting, "Teacher, don't you care that we're going to
drown?"

When Jesus woke up, he rebuked the wind and
said to the waves, "Silence! Be still!" Suddenly the
wind stopped, and there was a great calm. Then he
asked them, "Why are you afraid? Do you still have
no faith?"

MARK 4:37-40

God revealed that Christy had been trying to save her
family and herself through her own strength. Christy asked
Jesus for help, pledging her faith in Him regardless of life's
storms. Slowly, their family began to settle into their new life.
As Christy's emotions calmed, she began to see how much
Emily actually helped them all *stay* focused on Jesus.

In *A Grace Revealed*, Jerry Sittser writes, "[God] wants to
use the harsh conditions of life to shape us—and eventually
the whole world—into something extraordinarily beautiful."[4]

Redemption isn't a one-time thing! Yes, there is redemption of souls when we come to Jesus, but God also redeems
relationships. He redeems sinfulness and makes us clean
again (Psalm 51). He redeems time lost, unmet expectations,
and faithlessness (Joel 2:23-25).

For Christy's family, God eventually prompted them to
adopt a little girl with special needs from Ukraine. How's that
for redemption? A mother who nearly drowned in the waves
of fear when she first faced disability swims out to sea and
offers a lifeline to another child with special needs.

A Heart Revealed

Life is unpredictable, no matter how hard we try to maintain control, developing Plan A, Plan B, and Plan C. Proverbs 16:9 says, "We can make our plans, but the LORD determines our steps." Your family and your situation may be different, but perhaps you recognize the agony of letting go of the dreams you once cherished. Maybe you're still holding on to what you *thought* life would look like. Maybe you're still asking, *Why me?* God can handle our questions and cries for help!

Shauna Amick's daughter Sarah is now a spunky pre-teen, and God has redeemed her diagnosis in ways no one could have imagined. Shauna has become a disability-rights advocate and works for Joni and Friends, spending her life "speak[ing] up for those who cannot speak for themselves" (Proverbs 31:8). Shauna helps raise awareness of the genocide that is happening *in utero* to babies diagnosed with Down syndrome. Only a small percentage of these children have a chance at life, because as was the case with Sarah, most doctors recommend termination.[5]

"As my belly grew throughout my pregnancy, so did my heart for Sarah," Shauna says. "God showed his faithfulness by replacing my default tendency toward fear with a boldness to speak truth and live and love with new passion." On the day of Sarah's birth, when the delivery room doctor held her up for all to see, Shauna says she felt joy where fear had once reigned and honestly proclaimed, "She's beautiful."

Tests had revealed that Sarah was also going to be born with a heart defect, which is common with Down syndrome. Cardiologists hovered over Shauna as she delivered and whisked Sarah off to the neonatal intensive care unit.

"It didn't matter anymore that she had Down

syndrome," Shauna says. "I wanted to pull off all the cords and tubes that kept Sarah and me apart so I could hold her flesh-to-flesh."

It was a waiting game in the weeks after Sarah's birth as doctors tried to give her time to grow and make gains before undergoing the trauma of open-heart surgery. When Sarah could wait no longer, a specialist was called in, and she was prepped for surgery. Consent forms were signed, and the family settled in for a prayer-filled wait.

After a long day of waiting in a room full of weary and suffering parents, the Amicks were called in to speak with Sarah's surgeon.

"When I opened her up, it looked hopeless," the surgeon explained. "I didn't think I'd have anything to work with, but knock on wood, somehow I was able to repair her heart, and it is beautiful. She's as good as new!"

"It has nothing to do with knocking on wood," Shauna replied, breathing out a sigh of relief. "It's a miracle of God."

"Yes, it is a miracle!" he agreed.

Sarah has a deep appreciation for life, a compassion for others, and a true intimacy with Christ. Looking back, Shauna acknowledges that she was right about Sarah's life not being what she'd imagined for her child. "I praise God that because of Sarah, and yes, because of her disabilities, things have turned out better than we could have hoped or imagined!" (see Ephesians 3:20).

Have you presented the pieces of your heart to Jesus and asked Him to make it new? Read Ezekiel 36:26 with fresh eyes: "I will give you a new heart, and I will put a new spirit in you. I will take out your stony, stubborn heart and give you a tender, responsive heart."

A Heart Surrendered

Do you wonder what God's good plan for your child could possibly be? Have you questioned whether you made the right choice when you chose life, or do you find yourself wishing you'd been given the option to choose? If you chose to trust God and give your baby life, then you made the right choice. If you didn't have a choice, thank God for making the decision for you so you didn't have to agonize over it.

Your child was knit together in your womb for a purpose (Psalm 139:13-16). Comparing abilities and disabilities is a waste of time! The enemy of our souls wants us to view human life through a hierarchy of worth, with those affected by disability coming in at the bottom.

Michelle is the mother of two adult daughters with severe disabilities. She adopted them when they were babies. At the time of their adoption, Michelle knew there would be challenges ahead, but as the years went by and more and more diagnoses came to light, the magnitude of their family's situation became earth shattering.

"I dealt first with my infertility and then with my girls' diagnoses," Michelle explains. "I learned that as we mourn our dream child, our brokenness reveals the vast difference between our expectations and God's. It was brokenness and suffering that opened the door of my heart so that Jesus could enter in."

It's okay to cry out, "Why?!" It's okay to long for a different story. We can feel all of the normal emotions of anger and disappointment and grief. But we must arrive at the place of surrender where we accept God's story for our lives. When we do, He can take the fragile pieces of our broken hearts and put them back together with such tenderness that we're able to love with a supernatural, sacrificial love. That's when He gives us another kind of love—one that sees with heavenly eyes and loves as Jesus loves. We can trust that as hard as things may become, God has a purpose for the pain and a plan for good (Romans 8:28).

"God has not promised a state of constant bliss or a problem-free existence but has promised to be present in the silence and in the dark, to exist alongside us, within us, and for us," Yancey writes in *Reaching for the Invisible God.*[6]

Whatever diagnosis your child faces, or label a school district or professional has pronounced, remember that God has placed His stamp on your child—image bearer (Genesis 1:27). A soul is a soul, and your child's body contains a sacred one, created by God and destined to make a difference.

Journaling from the Heart

What affected you most from this chapter? Why? Were there elements that reminded you of your own story? If you haven't done so, pray and ask God to help you accept or grieve your child's disability and move forward in faith. Write your prayers. If some time has passed and you're in a different stage, pray for the mothers still coming to terms with their child's diagnosis, and thank God for His faithfulness.

6

A Joyful Heart:
Becoming Your Child's Biggest Fan

*"Mom, do you think I can do it? Do you think I can live by myself?"
Lisa wanted to know.*

"We won't know if you don't try," I answered.

*It was a mom answer for sure. It settled her, but not me. Was she
ready for this level of independence?*

*Standing in the living room of my daughter's small apartment,
memories of all that had brought us to her dream-come-true swirled
around in my mind. Lisa, twenty-six, was challenged by physical
and mental limitations that had been difficult and slow to diagnose.
When a heart infection ravaged her petite body and severely damaged
two heart valves, requiring a life-threatening surgery, we weren't sure
she would make it, much less ever be able to live on her own.*

*I had worked tirelessly to help her learn basic life skills.
Everything had to be sequenced, cued, and repeated countless times
with great consistency for Lisa to learn. Would she remember when
the time came to microwave a simple breakfast or make a cup of tea?
How would she do, alone all night? What could happen?*

*I knelt in front of Lisa as she sat in one of her new chairs with
a look of apprehension on her face. I took her small hands in mine
and prayed a prayer of blessing over her, her apartment, and the new
phase of her journey. When I finished, we were both in tears.*

DEBBIE SALTER GOODWIN—MOTHER OF LISA[1]

WHETHER IT'S A FIRST APARTMENT or first steps, moms make great cheerleaders. Smiling, with outstretched arms, moms build confidence with every "You can do it!"

But years of setbacks, overwhelming schedules, and unforeseen obstacles can slowly eat away at a cheery facade. What happens when we find ourselves feeling ill equipped and unsure of how to encourage or advocate for our special-needs child? Where can we find the strength to not just go on but also to be the real-deal, joy-filled mommas God calls us to be in Philippians 4:4—"Always be full of joy in the Lord. I say it again—rejoice!"?

You might be tempted to say, *Yeah, right!* and think this verse is simply unrealistic or unattainable in the daily struggles of special-needs parenting. The truth is that you'd be wrong. While the challenges and stress may seem overwhelming, and there may be days we need to have a good cry, our peace and joy are not dependent on our circumstances.

Laurie Wallin is a mother of four children, two of whom have special needs. In her book *Get Your Joy Back: Banishing Resentment and Reclaiming Confidence in Your Special Needs Family*, she writes about reaching her breaking point and realizing that God wants us to let go of resentment and bitterness and find real joy. "To do that will take something a lot stronger than we can muster through positive attitude, coping strategies, and punching the eighty-pound bag at the gym (although all of these do help!). No, it will take something much more powerful. Something supernatural, infinitely bigger than ourselves and the problems we and our kids face."[2]

Our Savior experienced this broken and hurting world so He could not only provide the path to righteousness but also leave us an example of faith in the face of unimaginable suffering. The author of Hebrews tells us we must fix our eyes on Jesus, remembering all that He endured on the Cross, so we "won't become weary and give up" (12:3). We must take our eyes off of our circumstances and look to the Source of all hope. "Rejoice in our confident hope. Be patient in trouble, and keep on praying" (Romans 12:12).

In her book *Choose Joy*, Kay Warren says joy is much more than happy feelings. "It's a settled assurance *about* God. A quiet confidence *in* God. And a determined choice to give our praise *to* God in all things. It means choosing joy again and again and again in the ups and downs, ins and outs of daily life."[3]

A Fearful Heart

Lisa has now lived on her own for more than fifteen years. Debbie has spent countless hours on her knees and learned some hard lessons about conquering fear and trusting God. She came to the realization that God knows Lisa's vulnerabilities better than she ever could.

The truth is that God knows each of our children—and each of us—better than we ever can. King David acknowledged, "O LORD, you have examined my heart and know everything about me. . . . Every day of my life was recorded in your book. Every moment was laid out before a single day had passed" (Psalm 139:1, 16).

Moms like to think that they're in control, but nothing shatters the illusion of control faster than having a child born with a disability.

As mothers, we like to think we are in control, especially when it comes to our families. But control is an illusion. And nothing shatters that illusion faster than having a child born with a disability.

Rachel Wilson, the mother of two children with regressive autism, writes about coming to terms with this reality in *The Life We Never Expected*, which she coauthored with her husband, Andrew:

> I am not the captain of this ship. I like to believe
> that I am and act as if I am, but I'm not. . . . We are,
> at best, sailing desperately into the fog, with ever-
> changing winds, choppy waters, blank maps, and no
> real idea what we're doing.
>   But God is the Captain. . . .
>   I can be confident that he will provide for us and
> for them. I know he will sustain us all. I know he
> will journey with us to the very end, at which point
> everything that is perishable and incomplete will be
> gloriously resurrected and healed.[4]

The Proverbs 31 woman exemplifies a mother who has learned to trust God, according to Kaylee Page, a blogger and special-needs mom.

> "Strength and dignity are her clothing, and she
> smiles at the future." Proverbs 31:25 . . .
>   The version I read years ago said "laughs at the
> days ahead." How odd, I thought. How can you
> laugh at what you don't know. It took me a while to
> realize that this woman, this Proverbs 31 woman, had
> a deep trust and understanding that God was and is
> in control. . . . It's a laughter that's like a "Ha, only
> you, God. Only you could make this story beautiful,

funny, unbearable, full of suffering and sorrow, but amazing, and honest and good, and weird, and humorous and comical and full of miracles."[5]

A Heart Revealed

Sometimes we get the message that good parents aren't supposed to struggle. Gillian Marchenko,[6] a special-needs mom and author of *Still Life: A Memoir of Living Fully with Depression*, says the bar is usually higher for Christian mothers. "We're supposed to handle biting, slapping, outbursts, embarrassing situations, stares, and rejection, all with an easy, winning smile and grace." Gillian says that moms are often afraid to be vulnerable and admit they need help.

Special-needs moms are not immune to society's pressure to "have it all together," according to Gillian. "Asking for help and support, especially long term, is uncomfortable. In this day and age, a lot of people don't even know the names of their neighbors next door. Relying on others has become unnatural. You don't *bother* people for help. You do what you need to do for yourself. Anything else is countercultural. Moms need to keep it together *and* do everything well. I often feel embarrassed because I can't seem to do everything I should be doing on my own."

We need to be brave enough to honestly share about how we are doing, be willing to ask for help, and cultivate a community of women who want to be authentic. We must also encourage our children to be vulnerable and take chances. They won't always succeed, and we may even be embarrassed, but they will be stretched as they take risks and learn to trust God for themselves.

Debbie remembers the day Lisa announced she believed

God wanted her to collect one hundred coats for needy children in their community. The idea seemed far-fetched, and Debbie began to list all of the reasons why the task wasn't realistic for Lisa. "That's when God shut my mouth just like He shut the mouths of the lions before Daniel. All of a sudden, I knew that God had a purpose and that I had better cooperate. I didn't take over any part of it, as I was prone to do to ensure Lisa's success. I somehow knew I was to watch from the sidelines."

Lisa collected coats, and stories of how God was working began to filter back to Debbie. Agencies that were reticent to trust others trusted Lisa with their donated coats. One church had inherited a clothes closet from a sister church and agreed to give Lisa the children's coats for her collection.

Lisa's confidence grew as she devised a reverse number chart so she would always know how many more coats she needed. By the time she had fifty coats, her friends and coworkers started to help. Lisa not only ended up reaching her goal but also exceeded it. God's final confirmation of His blessing on Lisa's mission came when the director of the collection center shared that because of the economic downturn, their agency would not have had coats for children that year without Lisa's efforts. Debbie learned that God wanted to use Lisa, and she could not interfere, even under the guise of protecting her daughter.

Sandi Anderson has two adult sons on opposite ends of the autism spectrum. Jerad is introverted, nonverbal, and prefers quiet; Joel is determined to travel the world speaking, sharing his artwork, and challenging assumptions.[7] Sandi has had to learn different ways to encourage and advocate according to each son's bent. Joel's big dreams have taken them to China to encourage orphans; Canada to serve as autism ambassadors alongside Temple Grandin (an agriculture professor and autism spokesperson); and Cape Town, South Africa. Sandi supported Joel through the process of writing and illustrating a children's book and helped him launch a website to sell his artwork. Their family has also started Jeremiah's Ranch, a program for adults living with disabilities.

Sandi says she realized early on that she would have to trust in God's purpose for her boys and ignore the limitations the world would try to place on them. Many times she's had to fight back her own fear and feelings of incompetence, looking to 2 Corinthians 12:9, where Paul teaches that all we need is God's grace, because His "power works best in weakness."

"God uses me like Gideon, not letting my fears stop Him from using Joel and Jerad," Sandi says. "I've learned that I can't sit back and wait for others to make things happen. I muster up the courage to do what God has asked me to do. I let my boys be vulnerable out in front of people, having patience with people no matter how unkind their responses may be, and even with family members who have shunned us.

"I used to say, 'outwit, outlast, outplay' and I would win 'survivor autism mom.' But I've realized that I don't want to just survive; I want to thrive along with my sons and husband. So I lean into Christ, who gives me endurance, patience, and joy."

A Heart Surrendered

If you are a music lover, perhaps you've heard of the virtuoso violinist Itzhak Perlman. Polio stole the strength of his legs, but fans don't focus on what his legs can't do. They focus on Perlman's flawless violin-playing technique and his unparalleled talent as a musician.

Have you spent too many years focusing on what's

broken—either in you or your children—instead of what works? Children with special needs face many barriers, and they need our encouragement, especially when it comes to learning to trust God—because their faith works.

Debbie says helping Lisa have a personal relationship with her Creator was her number one priority. "I always tried to help Lisa understand that God would speak to her directly. I didn't want her to confuse my voice and God's voice. Nor did I want her to believe that God would speak to her only through another person. I regularly nurtured the idea that if she listened and learned to discern how God spoke to her, she would never be alone."

When she and her husband realized that Lisa's challenges were going to be lifelong, they vowed to pray for her spiritual health first and foremost, even before physical healing. Debbie recalls,

> God answered our prayers over and over again.
> Lisa's heart—not the biological, life-giving pump
> that has failed her more than once, but the one God
> shaped and grew—is not disabled. It is as whole
> as it needs to be for her to follow God. I will never
> forget a conversation we had when I was trying to
> affirm Lisa for using God's gift of compassion to reach
> out to people who were surprised by her sensitivity.
> I was trying to tell her that God was using her in
> spite of her limitations. Her reply stunned me: "But
> Mom, my heart isn't disabled." It was truth, clear and
> unadorned. This same girl, who always fell below the
> norm on reading comprehension tests, could read
> God's Word and share insights that defied every IQ
> test. Lisa was right—her heart was not disabled.

While Lisa's physical heart did fail in 2016, her spiritual heart went home to be with the God she loved and served.

Wherever you find yourself today as a special-needs mom, remember that God sees your daily sacrifices. He knows if you're weary or struggling to find joy in the midst of it all. He wants to lift up your chin to take your eyes off your circumstances and remind you that you are His and He is good.

Kay Warren set out on her search for true joy after years of struggling with depression and losing her son to mental illness. "For joy to become a reality, you must fight against the heart attitudes of legalism, worry, workaholism, and perfectionism and instead nurture grace, trust, balance, and acceptance. It won't come without a struggle, but nothing worthwhile ever does. Once you and I become adept at nurturing joy in ourselves, we will find delight in nurturing it in others as well."[8]

The giant sequoia trees provide a valuable lesson on nurturing one another. While you might think these mammoth trees growing as tall as a thirty-story building would require a deep root system, the truth is that their roots are quite shallow. They survive the force of winds and rains because sequoias only grow in groves, with roots intertwined to provide support and sustenance.[9]

Lord, help us to follow the example of your creation,
finding sisters willing to practice interdependence so
we can point each other back to You and the real joy
available for us and our children.

Journaling from the Heart

What affected you most from this chapter? Why? Were there elements that reminded you of your own story? Pray and ask God to reveal any areas where you can do a better job encouraging your child. Ask God to bring you like-minded friends who want to be authentic so that you may come alongside one another, finding joy amid daily struggles.

7

A Nurturing Heart:
Keeping Marriage and Family United

"Mmm, just the way I like it," I declared, inhaling the steam rising from my cappuccino with just the right amount of foam.

The cool evening air of winter in Southern California welcomed us as we collapsed into the well-worn chairs on the front porch of our favorite coffeehouse. My husband, Steve, looked exhausted, and I didn't feel much better. He'd just returned from a long visit in Oklahoma to help with his ailing father, and I'd been left with our two young boys—one under a year old and the other with significant disabilities. We'd both been under immense pressure, and I was slowly feeling the stress lighten as we held hands and chatted in between sips.

Our reprieve was short lived as Steve hesitantly shared that his mother's call before we left for our date night was a call for help. His dad had taken a turn for the worse, and doctors feared the end was near. He needed to return to Oklahoma.

I wish I could say I was kind and understanding. I wish I could say I was calm and reassuring. I wish I could, but I can't. I needed my husband—his help, his support with our boys and their many needs. How could I possibly handle another absence so soon? My response came from a place of hurt and panic. Our date night ended with my husband feeling torn and overwhelmed as I juggled frustration, guilt, and regret.

MELISSA BUNDY—MOTHER OF CALEB[1]

THE WORD *NURTURE* may bring to mind images of cuddling or consoling a crying infant or bandaging a toddler's skinned knee. As a mother, nurturing is second nature for most of us—it's just what moms do. Our hearts are naturally drawn toward nurturing our children because they rely upon us and are dependent on us for their care. While nurturing a husband may not come as easily or naturally, a healthy marriage depends upon it.

When you nurture your spouse, you are caring for him. You are nourishing, protecting, and cherishing him. Although our original intent as we gaze into each other's eyes at the altar may be to protect and cherish our marriage, the daily demands of life, especially in a family impacted by disability, can make our vows hard to live out.

In the book *Married with Special-Needs Children: A Couples' Guide to Keeping Connected*, marriage is compared to a garden. No matter how beautiful and abundant the garden may start out, if it's not cared for—weeded, watered, fertilized—it will eventually succumb to the neglect and stop bearing fruit. "A beautiful garden can yield a bounty and serve as a refuge, but only if tended to over time," writes Dr. Laura Marshak.[2]

> Find time to hang out with your spouse. Admit that you don't have it all figured out and celebrate the love you share for one another and your family.

With doctor appointments and therapy visits, it can be difficult for parents of children with special needs to make their marriage a priority since there are already so many demands on their time. Couples may be tempted to view the investment as another task on an already long to-do list. Joe and Cindi Ferrini, however, know that making the marriage a priority will pay off.

"We have learned that a strong marriage is essential. Without it, caring for someone with special needs is that much more difficult and challenging," the Ferrinis wrote in an article for Focus on the Family addressing marriage and special needs.[3] After more than thirty-five years of marriage and caring for a grown son with cerebral palsy and intellectual disabilities, Joe and Cindi have some valuable insights for special-needs parents.

They encourage couples to embrace their new normal through keeping communication open and planning together as a team. Joe and Cindi caution couples about holding on to expectations of what their lives would have looked like rather than embracing the new and sometimes difficult realities of parenting a child with disabilities: "When we don't get what we want or expect, when our desires are not fulfilled, when we don't deal with the hurt and conflict properly, that's when our unrealistic expectations often lead to a lack of fulfillment in our relationships. The result is conflict and anger, possibly even divorce."[4]

If we're clear about our expectations, we can determine how realistic they are and help our spouses understand our perspective. It is unreasonable to think our spouses should simply know in advance how to meet our needs. If we want to be on the same page, functioning as teams, we need to discuss these unexpressed expectations.

A Fearful Heart

Teamwork can be challenging for couples parenting children with special needs because one spouse is usually the primary caregiver—typically the mom—and the husband may bear a huge responsibility to provide for the family financially. Without good communication and clear goals, there is potential for division.

Anna thought her husband, Tom, was being unreasonable. She was the one who spent every day with their daughter. She was the one who left playgroup feeling embarrassed because there was yet another milestone that other kids had passed as their daughter Katie lagged behind. Anna felt guilty for her feelings of embarrassment because she knew Katie's delays resulted from her autism. *Why won't Tom just agree to pay for the additional therapy?* she wondered.

Anna knew Tom's answer. They simply couldn't afford additional therapy and the overload on Katie's appointment schedule while also managing their other children's activities. Even though she understood his rationale and couldn't argue with the numbers, somehow Anna blamed Tom and continued to question the choice: *What if Katie continues to get further and further behind?—will they still let her start school next year? How can we not do everything possible to help our child?* Constantly rehearsing the what-ifs and worst-case scenarios left Anna filled with anxiety. First Peter 3:5-6 paints a clear picture of what trusting God looks like, even in times of fear:

> This is how the holy women of old made themselves beautiful. They put their trust in God and accepted the authority of their husbands. For instance, Sarah obeyed her husband, Abraham, and called him her master. You are her daughters when you do what is right without fear of what your husbands might do.

Pastor and author John Piper, in his book *This Momentary Marriage*, explains that fear gives way when we place our trust in God: "The daughters of Sarah fight the anxiety that rises in their hearts. They wage war on fear, and they defeat it with hope in the promises of God."[5]

Piper points out that biblical submission does not mean we agree with our husbands on everything or fail to share our own wisdom and perspective. He describes it as "the divine calling of a wife to honor and affirm her husband's leadership and help carry it through according to her gifts."[6]

Anna shared her frustration with a close friend she'd met through Katie's special-needs class at church. The two moms met for lunch, and after listening intently, her friend agreed that while the therapy could possibly help Katie, it would also take a toll on their already overstretched family. Anna heeded her advice and eventually let go of her desire to try the additional therapy, as well as her resentment of Tom.

Helpful Tips for Couples

After interviewing numerous parents of children with special needs, the writers for the Enabled Kids website found one pronounced, unifying thread: having friends and a supportive network is crucial for a family's health. Close friends and extended family may offer practical help, advice, or just camaraderie in the day-to-day struggles. Here is their list of tips for couples.

1. Set aside time every day to chat one-on-one.
2. Preserve intimacy.
3. Face challenges of your child as a team.
4. Stick to the positives.
5. Be around a supportive community. [7]

Note the recommendation to be around a supportive community. Although there is a wealth of personal stories and helpful advice available through different blogs and online groups, these cannot take the place of personal, face-to-face connections.

Churches can provide a lifeline for hurting families that often feel isolated and alone. Marisol and her daughter, Meghan, were accustomed to being stared at in the mall, where few identified with a seventeen-year-old in a wheelchair. Meghan's birth defect caused reduced mobility in many of her joints. However, their lives changed for the better when they found a church with special-needs support groups for parents and a youth group that quickly welcomed and included Meghan. Marisol and her husband found great comfort in getting to know other couples that shared similar fears and concerns for their children.

When marriages don't survive, single parents can especially benefit from a caring support group at church that understands their tangible needs. A single mother of three children, including one with autism, tears up at the realization that while she needs God more than ever, she hasn't taken her children to church in some time. "Church is hard," she says, explaining that her son's outbursts embarrass his siblings. Although no one from her church has ever reached out to her, this mom believes they would try to help if she asked. But like many single parents, she doesn't ask, which deprives people of the blessing of being more like Jesus. Remember, giving and receiving are big parts of being a family, especially the family of God.

A Heart Revealed

Mothers of children with disabilities become well versed at understanding their child's communication style and how they express their needs. The ears of a momma quickly interpret what may sound like garble or grunts to anyone else. Time and attentiveness help us learn our children's different nuances in communication. It's born of necessity—life goes more smoothly when we understand each other.

The same is true for our marriages. If we're honest, most of us haven't spent nearly enough time paying attention to our spouse's communication style. We are not as intentional in observing and learning what "makes them tick" as we are with our children. This may be because we don't have to worry about our husbands throwing a fit in the grocery store aisle! Much as we've learned how to set up our children for success, we should do the same for our marriages.

Dr. Gary Chapman, bestselling author and speaker for marriage conferences nationwide, challenges couples to nurture their marriages by learning what communicates love to their spouses—their love languages. In his book *The Five Love Languages*, he writes, "Isolation is devastating to the human psyche. That is why solitary confinement is considered the cruelest of punishments. At the heart of mankind's existence is the desire to be intimate and to be loved by another. Marriage is designed to meet that need for intimacy and love."[8]

To express love in a way our husbands will best be able to receive it, Chapman asserts that we must know our husband's love language. "In the context of marriage, if we do not feel loved, our differences are magnified," Dr. Chapman teaches. "We come to view each other as a threat to our happiness. We fight for self-worth and significance, and marriage becomes a battlefield rather than a haven."[9]

Just as we become experts when it comes to learning our children's communication cues, we must take the time to learn how our husbands receive and return love. We need to look for the indicators that tell us they may be hurting and need a break or time to talk. This requires patience, understanding, and a choice to be intentional about our interactions.

A Heart Surrendered

After more time and more breakdowns in communication, it became clear to Melissa and Steve that they needed help to strengthen their marriage.

"We began to see that we were not nurturing our marriage," Melissa says. "We finally realized we needed to seek professional counseling. As an ordained pastor, it was very humbling for my husband to admit that he needed help—that his marriage was struggling."

Melissa describes that difficult season of their marriage as a time of painful pruning. When a garden has been neglected, one of the first steps is to cut off the overgrowth and dead branches to encourage new growth.

For special-needs families that face stares, glares, and misunderstandings from the outside world, the tendency can be for one or both parents to begin to isolate themselves. This can lead to an unhealthy level of dependency upon one another.

"I could see that I had begun to lean way too much on Steve as my strength, my stability. We were not looking to Christ as the Source for our strength and the unconditional love we needed for our sons and for each other," Melissa says.

Melissa and Steve sought godly counsel, and as part of that process, they created a "Marriage Manifesto" to clearly outline how their goals and priorities for their family would be lived out. Since quality time is a love language they share, one of the key items was a commitment to spend more time alone together.

The Manifesto includes a specific number of date nights per month and a certain number of weekend getaways for the two of them. Melissa says other wives have asked her from time to time how they can afford to have such frequent date nights.

"How can you afford not to?" Melissa responds. "We see this as necessary for keeping our marriage healthy and producing fruit. We recognize that not everyone will be able to have dates out of the house or nights away. There are still many times when we are unable to get away, and we'll have 'date night in.' While it's not perfect, we pick up our favorite takeout and create a romantic setting to allow us to focus on each other."

As Melissa and Steve reflect on those years when their marriage had become a neglected landscape, they praise God for bringing them to the point of surrendering their relationship to Him. They learned to depend upon Christ's strength for their marriage and to help them in the daily struggles of special-needs parenting. Their little boys are now strapping teenagers; their son who requires a wheelchair has never spoken a word.

"[Your marriage] can actually grow deeper because you are walking through a journey that brings a lot of suffering," Steve says. "When you learn to embrace one another in that journey and walk through it together, it can actually strengthen your marriage."[10]

On a cool winter evening, they can still be found sitting together on the front porch of their favorite coffeehouse. They have loved and nurtured each other through birth, death, and diagnoses. They'll be the first to admit that they may not have it all figured out, but they are still in love, and they're still a family.

Journaling from the Heart

What affected you most from this chapter? Why? Have you considered areas where you can do a better job of nurturing intimacy within your marriage? If you haven't done so, pray and ask God to give you wisdom about prioritizing your marriage and communicating love to your spouse. Write down your thoughts.

_____

_____

_____

_____

_____

_____

_____

_____

_____

_____

_____

_____

_____

_____

_____

_____

_____

_____

_____

_____

_____

_____

8

A Trusting Heart:
Sharing Christ When Setbacks Come

"Mom!" Steve called out with panic in his voice.

"What is it?"

"These merit-badge instructions make no sense!" he exclaimed. "I think I'm going to have to do all twelve weeks of fitness training all over again! I can't do this!"

My son's anger and frustration had boiled over by the time I made it to his room. His head was in his hands, and the meticulous records he'd kept for the past twelve weeks were strewn on the floor.

Steve had been inching his way through the ranks of Boy Scouts for three years, dreaming of becoming an Eagle Scout. This was a big dream for any boy, especially one diagnosed with attention deficit disorder (ADD) and dyslexia. That morning he discovered he had incorrectly measured his fitness, flexibility, and strength before starting, so the grueling weeks of training wouldn't count. He would have to start over.

He fumed for hours, occasionally shouting, "This is impossible!" Steve finally quieted down, but his frustration was still evident. My heart was breaking for him. I silently prayed he wouldn't drop out.

KATHY KUHL—MOTHER OF STEVE[1]

❦

WITNESSING YOUR CHILD'S regular setbacks is disheartening and frustrating, especially when the special need is not readily observable. Children with disabilities such as ADD, autism spectrum disorders, emotional disorders, mental illness, learning disabilities, and chronic fatigue syndrome (to name a few) may look the same as others, but they face tremendous invisible challenges. Learning to trust God and allow Him to work in the midst of setbacks isn't easy, especially when others don't "see" or understand your child's disability.

Parents of children with invisible disabilities face many of the same daily challenges, setbacks, and fears of the future as families affected by other disabilities. They may not, however, have the same level of support or understanding from family, friends, or even bystanders.

"The more 'invisible' the disability, the easier it is to dismiss," wrote Sarah Parshall Perry in a blog entitled "Invisible Diagnoses and the God Who Sees."[2]

Special dietary requests can be seen as over the top. Rigid schedules and therapy plans may be viewed as excessive. And as a result, mothers can be left feeling hurt and misunderstood.

Jamie watched her son Elijah from the park bench, trying to give him space to explore and play with the other kids. Her peace was gone in an instant when another boy decided to snatch away the tiny plastic shovel they had brought from home. Elijah exploded, lashing out at the other boy, hitting and screaming. Jamie wanted to correct her child, but she knew he couldn't process it while he was so angry. She knelt down and wrapped her arms around him in a firm hug to help calm him down. Jamie could practically feel the stares of every parent at the playground. She knew they thought Elijah should have been disciplined instead of comforted—some even expressed it.

A Fearful Heart

Sarah is the mother of two sons with autism and numerous other hidden disabilities. Her eleven-year-old, Noah, has been diagnosed with Disruptive Mood Dysregulation Disorder (DMDD), which is akin to childhood bipolar disorder. Yet her beautiful brood may look picture perfect.

One time, after a particularly stressful day, Noah became so emotionally distraught that he attempted to throw himself out of their moving vehicle. He was yanking on his seatbelt, saying he didn't want to live, and he opened his door while on the freeway.

"Please, God," Sarah prayed that night, "whatever hurts me, I will take a double portion, so that Noah will hurt less."

Worry and anxiety seem to come naturally with motherhood, so how can we simply let go and trust?

Sarah finds solace in 1 Peter 5:7: "Give all your worries and cares to God, for he cares about you."

What if we viewed trusting as laying down our anxieties and fears at the feet of the One who gave our children breath, the Creator who entrusted them to *us*? We need to remind ourselves of Jesus' call in Matthew 11:28-30—He knows our weary hearts, and He tells us to lay down our heavy burdens and seek His will and His plan for our families.

Sarah has come to the place where she can acknowledge that although she probably wouldn't have chosen their difficult path, she's learned to trust that God sees her family's struggles, and His plan is best.

In the early years of learning to navigate Steve's ADD diagnosis, Kathy couldn't have imagined how God's plans for them would not only enable her son to succeed but also lead her down a new career path. By third grade, Steve was struggling to keep up in school. His Individualized Education Program (IEP) wasn't working for him. Each day, Steve came home from school tired and frustrated, and he was starting to think he couldn't learn. Kathy and her husband began to research private schools.

When no other options panned out, Kathy decided to try homeschooling Steve. With much trepidation and prayer, the two set out on their new adventure at the beginning of his fourth-grade year. Through homeschooling, Kathy was able to find creative ways to help Steve catch up on his reading and handwriting. She also figured out how to help him stay focused on learning.

"I let him move," Kathy says. "He would bounce on a minitrampoline while reviewing math facts, practice spelling using chalk on the driveway, solve math problems while stretched out under the dining room table. Homeschooling let us nurture his talents instead of focusing on what he couldn't do or the constant setbacks."

During their first few months of homeschooling, Kathy discovered a quotation from Charles Spurgeon that symbolized her son's striving. The great Baptist preacher said, "By perseverance, the snail reached the ark." Kathy encourages parents to remember that for some children, to just keep trying *is* heroic.[3]

For some children, to just keep trying *is* heroic.

Kathy acknowledges that there were times when Steve wanted to quit and days when she envied the mothers who put their kids on a bus and seemed to have an easier time of it. But whenever they weighed the options, homeschooling was clearly the best choice for their son's academic success.

Since Steve graduated nearly ten years ago, Kathy has traveled the country speaking and sharing from her experiences, and she also writes about homeschooling and how to help children with special needs overcome their unique challenges.

A Heart Revealed

As mothers, our natural tendency is to want to protect our children from life's pain and hardships. We will go above and beyond to get help, find a solution, or know everything we can about a condition. A mother can be her child's strongest advocate—and rightfully so. However, we must also remember that there are lessons to be learned through trials and disappointments.

James 1:2-4 assures us that setbacks can actually be an "opportunity for great joy" because our children can learn endurance and perseverance. It can be agonizing to stand back and not intervene, but there are times we must let our children work through an issue or trial.

Cassandra's thirteen-year-old daughter, Cami, has sensory processing disorders, plus multiple learning differences and mild ADD. Although Cami's hidden disabilities make tasks more difficult, her mother is trying to fight the instinct to jump in and ease her daughter's frustrations.

She knows that rescuing Cami can actually impede her growth and progress in the long run, but it's hard nevertheless. In a blog post, Cassandra wrote about her struggle to stop being an overprotective "helicopter mom": "I know this truth in my head, but in those moments of struggle, my momma's heart hurts for her. I just want to fix it, so her way will be a little easier. Yet in my efforts to ensure her success, I am setting her up to fail. And I'm getting in God's way in her life."[4]

When our children's troubles threaten to overwhelm us, we have to turn to what we know from God's Word. Do we believe that God rules and that He is wise and loving? If so, then He must have a good purpose in allowing these difficulties in our lives.

It's like a mother forcing a small child to swallow medicine that tastes yucky: She knows it will help, but the child doesn't understand. Children must learn to trust their parents and obey, even when things don't make sense.

We, too, face the choice of whether to accept what God gives. Like a sick child, will we swallow the unpleasant medicine, or will we fight and spit? Proverbs 3:5-6 reminds us to "trust in the LORD" rather than depend on our own understanding of our circumstances. We often can't understand why God allows the adversity and challenges our kids must face. It's okay to cry out to Him with our frustrations, but ultimately we must trust that God "disciplines those he loves" like a parent with a child (Hebrews 12:6).

In his book *Learning to Soar*, Avery Willis writes about the maturation process for eagles, comparing it to how God treats his children. He details how the parents slowly wean the eaglets from their protection and provision so they can live up to their full potential. Mistakes and setbacks are part of the process when learning to fly. Just as a young eagle must decide if it's ready to try again, Willis says we, too, face a crisis of belief when we face trials and setbacks. "God wants to develop your faith from experience to experience until you trust him in every situation."[5]

Our faith in action is a powerful model for our children. However, they must recognize God's love and learn to take their own steps of faith, according to their abilities and understanding. In Matthew 19:14, Jesus invited *all* children to come to Him, and He is still doing it today.

For more helpful information on how children with special needs can grow in their faith, visit www .joniandfriends.org/real-families-real-needs.

A Heart Surrendered

Parenting children with special needs can be discouraging, especially when it seems that with every two steps forward, there are three steps back. King Solomon understood that hope deferred can make our hearts sick (Proverbs 13:12). He also cautions us to guard our hearts because "it determines the course" our lives will take (Proverbs 4:23). To guard our hearts, we must feed our souls.

This can seem impossible during the stress and aftermath of a crisis or setback. But if we've made personal prayer and Bible reading a priority, we'll have a strong foundation to depend on. The hard work we've done to feed our souls and root ourselves in God's Word will sustain us during the harder times when we can barely lift our heads. There will be days when we can only manage a few bleary-eyed minutes of Bible reading and snippets of prayer. Memorizing Scripture stocks our heads and hearts with verses to fall back on when long vigils interrupt our routines, and singing hymns can also bring comfort during tumultuous times.

Remember, it's okay to cry and express our heartache and disappointment to our heavenly Father. We don't need to pretend to be happy all the time. We weep for our kids. We feel deeply their pain and struggles. We lament when they've lost ground or must start over. We ache for our children when other kids are cruel. We grieve for the death of our dreams.

When we let go of the life we imagined, God doesn't require us to do it stoically, as if it cost us nothing.

Sometimes, we cry with a new diagnosis. While a diagnosis can be a relief, it can also bring a flood of new questions, worries, specialists, treatments, and medications. Sometimes our children receive different diagnoses as they grow, and that news can hurt. Suddenly we have a new set of specialists, vocabulary, therapies, and acronyms to master, a new prognosis to come to terms with or question.

The key is not to get stuck in our sorrow. "Weeping may last through the night, but joy comes with the morning" (Psalm 30:5). A big part of being able to face the next day's challenges is our ability to look for the good and give thanks. Even in times of sorrow, God has given us so much. How easy it is to continue along the way and not stop to acknowledge all the ways God moves throughout our days, like nine of the ten lepers Jesus healed in Luke 17. We must turn back and fall at His feet. Giving thanks is not a magic spell that fixes our troubles. Instead, giving thanks is part of how God adjusts our attitudes and our focus onto the eternal and onto His provision, His care.

We can be like selfish children at a birthday party, ignoring a dozen lavish gifts we needed—perhaps even gifts we asked for. But we stand pouting because some other thing we wanted is missing. So in times of setback, sit down and make a list, if that helps you. What can you sincerely give thanks for: Food? A good roof? A relative who cares about you? A job? That your child is still alive? That your son smiled today? Maybe you are just glad your daughter didn't get sick again today—give thanks for that! There is always something to give thanks for. We can *choose* a grateful perspective and celebrate opportunities along the way.

Steve Kuhl discovered this as he set out on his second attempt at earning his physical fitness badge for Boy Scouts. After grumbling for a few days about the evils of the detailed requirements, he picked up a pencil and started a new set of initial measurements and another round of intense exercise for twelve weeks. By the end of the first week, he had stopped complaining about having to do it over. By the end of the twelve weeks, he was preaching the value of the fitness program. "Mom!" he proclaimed, "everybody in America needs to do this merit badge!"

Steve also discovered that a two-mile run in the morning before he and his mom started homeschooling made it easier for him to focus on his work. He said it gave him time to think of everything that would typically be running through his mind while he was supposed to be working.

Kathy watched as her son's struggle built up his already incredible perseverance. And having conquered what was the hardest merit badge for him, Steve kept going. Despite dyslexia, he inched through all the complex requirements for the remaining badges. Despite attention deficit disorder, he used his excellent people skills to manage a volunteer staff of more than fifty at Great Falls National Park—the largest volunteer project ever held there. Despite auditory processing difficulties, he passed the oral exams for his Eagle Board of Review. Steve became an Eagle Scout, an honor achieved by only one scout in a hundred. He still presses on, through college and other challenges.

When we press on despite obstacles, we show our children how, by God's grace, they, too, can move on and achieve goals that can astonish the experts and maybe even surprise themselves. Sometimes our children's accomplishments are unexpected successes. But not always. Sometimes, the victory is just in picking themselves up to try again. We can help them learn to run with endurance the race set before them (see Hebrews 12:1), confident in the One who sets our path, weeps with us in our sorrows, and prods us on.

Journaling from the Heart

What affected you most from this chapter? Why? Think of some setbacks your family has experienced. Do you wish you had handled them differently? In what ways did your child learn and grow from the experience? Consider how you might respond differently the next time you see a child acting out who doesn't appear to have a disability.

PART 3

A Sibling's Journey

9
Realities for Siblings

Twelve-year-old Allison slammed her bedroom door and clicked the lock just before her older brother started banging on it. Her heart pounded as she gulped for breath and replayed the scene in her mind.

She had simply walked past Roger while he was dancing to a Disney movie. Before she knew what was happening, he pushed her so hard that she fell against a chair, briefly knocking the wind out of her. Then Roger struck two blows to Allison's back before she reached the safety of her room.

With tears streaming down her cheeks, Allison cried out, "Why does his autism *make* my *life so hard? How are we supposed to live like this? Please, God, do something!"*

❧

As a parent of children with and without disabilities, you have a unique role—and some distinct challenges. For many siblings, growing up alongside a brother or sister with disabilities can be an enjoyable and deeply rewarding experience. Others, like Allison, have carried emotional and even physical wounds for years. Their feelings of anger, hurt, resentment, and confusion are realities that must be faced—but not alone!

With God on your side, there is much you can do to

help siblings thrive amid unique challenges. In the next four chapters, you'll discover some common experiences, inspiring Bible promises, and practical suggestions to help you navigate some of the issues siblings face.

All of the children in a family are directly affected when one member has a disability. But when so much of the parents' time must be devoted to caring for a child with disabilities, some siblings can be left feeling alone and misunderstood. Other siblings may be able to take the challenges in stride and view their brother's or sister's disability as a family mission.

Whether the experience of your nondisabled children falls more toward one end or the other of this spectrum, or somewhere in between, they will benefit from connecting with others who understand their journeys and want to help strengthen their faith. You can help in three specific ways:

- *Be proactive.* There are a couple of practical steps your family can take to ensure everyone's safety and comfort. If physically abusive situations arise, it can be helpful for your nondisabled child to have a "safe space" somewhere in your home where he can go while his sibling is upset. Also, it can be especially valuable for him to have a chance to "debrief" with you after an instance in which his sibling has hurt him. If this is not already a normal practice in your family, take the initiative to implement it the next time this sort of circumstance arises. Your nondisabled children need to know that you, their parent, are doing everything in your power to protect and keep them safe—and that they're not alone in this challenging situation.

- *Be encouraging and comforting.* One of the most beautiful descriptions of God's unique plan for each person is found in Psalm 139:13-16. The psalmist assures us that God is intimately involved in creating each child in the womb. Before each of us was born, God had already laid out every moment and day of our lives.

When Moses tried to use his speech impediment as an excuse and questioned whether God could use him, God responded, "Who makes a person's mouth? Who decides whether people speak or do not speak, hear or do not hear, see or do not see? Is it not I, the LORD?" (Exodus 4:11).

Just as God has a specific purpose for your child with a disability, He also has a divinely ordained plan for your nondisabled child. You and your children can trust that no one is ever a mistake, afterthought, or surprise to God!

• *Be directive.* Like Allison, your children may be struggling to process why they are going through such painful circumstances and how it can really be part of God's plan. You can remind them that since God has specific, well-thought-out plans for each individual person, this also means that He has specific plans for entire families—including yours! He divinely selected those individuals who would comprise each family, including the brothers and sisters that each of you would have. So when your nondisabled child feels confused or alone, it's important for him to remember that God intentionally arranged and is continually active in his specific family situation, down to the last detail. When he's tempted to yearn for a sibling without paralysis, speech difficulties, fragile health issues, or autism, gently remind him of God's love and sovereignty.

Supporting Your Nondisabled Child

Two-child families in which one child has a disability and the other doesn't can be even more susceptible to a variety of thorny issues. Without other brothers or sisters to relate with, the negative feelings of your nondisabled child may be compounded, particularly her feelings of isolation. These feelings can be diminished through the support of friends and, especially, by helping her connect with others who have siblings with disabilities.

Don Meyer started the Sibling Support Project[1] more than twenty-five years ago because he recognized the unique needs of these siblings. In *The Sibling Survival Guide*, he recorded some of the insights he gleaned from working closely with siblings, including some of their own personal accounts. Many nondisabled brothers and sisters reported a sense of relief when they first realized they weren't alone in their journey and that others could relate to their experiences. From feelings of awe and inspiration to anger and resentment, similar themes show up in the contributions from siblings.

One sibling, for example, confesses resentment about how much her family's life has to revolve around her sister. From the vehicle they drive, to where they vacation, to how late they can stay out—much is dictated by the needs of the daughter with a disability. "I have never known anything else and I guess that makes it easier for me. Loving her and feeling she is the center of your world are two very separate things but something I can do very easily at once," she writes.[2]

Unfortunately, it's not always easy for children to keep feelings of bitterness and resentment from taking root in their hearts when their needs and wants almost always come second to those of the sibling with a disability. Even though they may understand the necessity of the situation, there can still be a sense of hurt.

Scripture teaches that negative feelings can easily lead to sinful attitudes and actions. In fact, the writer of Hebrews urges believers to help each other guard against these emotions. Hebrews 12:15 says, "Look after each other so that none of you fails to receive the grace of God. Watch out that no poisonous root of bitterness grows up to trouble you, corrupting many." This powerful imagery highlights just how dangerous bitterness (as well as anger and resentment) can be for a believer. If your child is feeling these emotions toward a brother or sister with a disability, forgiveness is a critical step of obedience and is important for his or her relationship with Christ. At the end of this chapter, you'll find some ideas for helping your child work through these emotions.

There are several ways you can help reduce or avoid resentment and bitterness. Connecting your child to other siblings of children with disabilities, planning special times with him, celebrating his accomplishments, and expressing your gratitude are a few ways to ease these feelings.

Maggie's little sister, Caitlin, is paralyzed, and for years she felt as though her parents showed favoritism toward Caitlin. She resented the extra attention Caitlin received and the special adaptive equipment they would purchase for her. It wasn't until Maggie's family attended a Joni and Friends Family Retreat that her heart changed. For the first time, Maggie met other siblings working through the same issues. She learned to view Caitlin with the eyes of Jesus and to understand her parents' struggles as well.[3]

Many parents have begun to realize the importance of being intentional about planning one-on-one time with each of their children, even if it's brief. If this isn't already happening in your family, this is a great way to begin showing your children, disabled and nondisabled alike, how deeply you appreciate them. Make a point of letting your nondisabled children know that you see the daily sacrifices they make and the patience they show toward their brother or sister. Reassure them that you're aware of just how many times they've not expected or even asked for something because the family budget is tight, and make it a point to acknowledge their willingness to help care for their sibling.

Sandra Peoples grew up with an older sister with Down syndrome and is now the mother of two boys, one with autism. In a blog for Key Ministry, she provides insights from both perspectives. "I tried to be perfect and low maintenance to make up for the extra work and attention my parents had to put into her," Sandra recalls about her own childhood. She reminds parents of the importance of celebrating all of their children's accomplishments and of expressing gratitude to their nondisabled child with statements such as "Thanks for holding your brother's hand to cross the street. Thanks for standing up for your sister when those kids weren't nice to her. Thank you for going to his favorite restaurant again."[4]

Changing Perspectives

For weeks, Santiago had tried to teach his twin brother how to play a new video game. But Agustín just didn't get it. Santiago sighed and walked away in frustration. Agustín was so different from other boys their age. Even their younger sisters, Daniella and Maria, could play this game with Santiago. But Agustín's fingers never pressed the right buttons at the right times. While Santiago really wanted to play with his brother, he had to admit that he was sick and tired of trying to help him. Why did his brother have to have Down syndrome? Why couldn't Agustín be like other kids instead of always needing so much extra help?

It's normal for your child to wish at times that her sibling with disabilities could do all the things that she and her friends can do. Both Allison and Santiago struggled well into their college years with questioning God and wondering what it would be like to have a brother without a disability. Allison often compared her family situation with that of her friends and sometimes resented not having a "normal" older brother. Similarly, Santiago was frustrated for many years that his brother's disability limited the activities they could do together. However, by God's grace, Allison and Santiago began to learn the truth about God's bigger plan, and it transformed their perspectives about their siblings.

Trusting God with Hidden Pain

Thirteen-year-old Hiroaki watched his parents and older brother, Kanaye, leave to head back to the mental health facility. Kanaye had been home from the facility for just three weeks before he had tried to commit suicide again. Their parents had sought treatment for him at the facility five times in eighteen months, and still Kanaye was unstable. Hiroaki wondered why God would create his brother with a chemical imbalance that would cause him to have such despairing thoughts. Would his brother ever get better? Would his parents ever be able to stop worrying about Kanaye's mental health?

Having a sibling with a mental illness can be especially challenging because it is a type of "invisible" disability, meaning that on the outside, a person with a mental illness looks no different from anyone else. However, the struggles that someone with mental illness faces are real, and these struggles affect the entire family. For example, Kanaye's depression made a deep impact on his parents and younger brother. Hiroaki constantly worried about whether his brother would succeed in committing suicide, and he also struggled with his faith.

Like Hiroaki, your nondisabled child may be questioning God's role in your family's situation. Above all, he needs to be reassured of God's sovereignty and promise of peace. He also needs to know that his sibling's mental illness is not anyone's fault—least of all his own. It's the result of a complex set of factors, often including a chemical imbalance in the brain. Depending on your child's degree of understanding, you may also need to ease his fears over whether he is in danger of contracting the mental illness. Reassure him that the Lord loves him and your entire family with a tender love, and that no matter how bleak things may seem now, there is still hope.

You and your family can find comfort and encouragement in knowing that God is in the process of redeeming your family's circumstances. While the term *redemption* is often used to describe Jesus' payment for our sins on the Cross, it can also describe how God brings something good from what began as a bad situation. Growing up with a sibling with disabilities can be tough, but God may be using the experience to refine your child's character, teach her to rely on His strength, or prepare her for a special ministry in the future. What feels like an overwhelming situation for her now may be one of the ways that God is growing her into the person He has called her to be.

Consider Tracy's story. Although Tracy's family had been attending Joni and Friends Family Retreats for several years, one summer God opened a new door of opportunity for her. Tracy was asked to co-lead a sibling-support workshop. After the workshop, Tracy said, "I'd never really considered God's role for me as a sibling until I was asked to do this."[5] It's amazing to think that ever since she was young, God was preparing her to minister to other siblings. In Jeremiah 29:11, God reminds us that He has specific plans for our lives; they are, He says, "plans for good and not for disaster, to give you a future and a hope."

In Ecclesiastes 3:11, we read, "He has planted eternity in the human heart, but even so, people cannot see the whole scope of God's work from beginning to end." While God knows what will happen throughout eternity, our perspective is limited. When life is frustrating and the future is uncertain, we must help our children learn to stand on the promises of God's Word.

> Your child may be having difficulty seeing how God could bring something good from your family's struggles. Look for a way to connect him or her with other "typical" siblings who have had more life experiences and opportunities to see God's redemption plan at work.

A Story of Redemption

The story of Joseph in the book of Genesis may be particularly encouraging to your nondisabled child. Joseph was just a teenager when his brothers turned against him and sold him into slavery. During his time in Egypt, Joseph was falsely accused and imprisoned. Although Joseph faced horrible circumstances during both his slavery and imprisonment, he honored God and rose to positions of leadership.

In Genesis 41, Joseph interprets Pharaoh's dreams and is promoted to serving as the second-in-command over all of Egypt. This promotion came thirteen years after Joseph's brothers had sold him. This long period of living as a slave and a prisoner was a refining time in Joseph's life. He learned leadership skills as he supervised other slaves and prisoners, and he learned to trust God.

In Genesis 45, Joseph affirms God's redemption of his situation by telling his brothers, "Don't be upset, and don't be angry with yourselves for selling me to this place. . . . God has sent me ahead of you to keep you and your families alive and to preserve many survivors" (Genesis 45:5, 7).

After their father dies, Joseph's brothers become concerned that Joseph might still hold a grudge against them. But Joseph explains to his brothers, "You intended to harm me, but God intended it all for good. He brought me to this position so I could save the lives of many people" (Genesis 50:20).

Just as Joseph's brothers treated him unfairly, your children may have been hurt—physically or emotionally—by their sibling with disabilities. Like Joseph, they may have spent many years in difficult situations, struggling to understand God's plan. But just as God redeemed Joseph, He can redeem your family's situation.

In their book *The Resilient Family: Living with Your Child's Illness or Disability*, Paul W. Power and Arthur E. Dell Orto emphasize that most children are resilient and will adapt and thrive within their unique family situations if their parents are proactive and aware of how they're affected.[6] With God's help and your loving guidance, growing up as a sibling of a child with disabilities can become, despite its challenges, a positive element of your child's life story.

Faith-Building for Siblings

If your nondisabled child is struggling with daydreaming or wishing for a different kind of life, encourage her to experiment with this three-step plan:

1. Ask God to help her see her sibling as someone who was wonderfully created by God.
2. Pray that God will help her love her brother or sister and focus on his or her abilities.
3. Thank God for being always in charge (sovereign) in her life and her family's daily life.

The following are some ideas you can share with your child to help him work through issues of forgiveness related to having a sibling with disabilities:

• Write a message to God explaining exactly what it is he's angry, bitter, or resentful about. Think through the different ways that his sibling has hurt him, physically or emotionally, and write these in a letter to God.
• Ask God to help him forgive his brother or sister for the specific things he has listed.

- Help him find a sibling support group or some blogs that would be appropriate. The Sibling Leadership Network[7] has numerous links to help him connect with other siblings.

10

Growing Up Too Fast

Seven-year-old Pranav immediately recognized Vihaan's epileptic seizure when his young brother's eyes rolled back into his head. Unfortunately, the muscle spasms and severe jerking had become all too familiar. Pranav's heart pounded as he quickly grabbed the phone and dialed 9-1-1.

Vihaan's seizure seemed to last longer this time, and their babysitter didn't know what to do. As Pranav recited his address to the emergency operator, he carefully watched Vihaan's breathing like he had seen his mother do to make sure his brother was still conscious. He didn't know what else to do except wait for help to arrive . . . and pray.

SIBLINGS OF CHILDREN with disabilities are often required to take on extra responsibilities and sometimes even assume an adult caregiver's role. Some report they feel pushed to grow up much faster than their peers and that they experience more anxiety and stress.[1] This chapter will explore some of the ways in which siblings have learned to cope with their brother's or sister's special needs at home, school, and church. Many have not only coped but also learned to thrive. With God's help, your "typical" children, too, can find strength—and even a sense of gratitude—for the unique situations they face every day.

Pranav's mature response to his brother's seizures may be surprising, but it can be beneficial for your children to learn to adapt to their sibling's unique health needs. Their fears and anxieties can be eased when they know what to do.

In a documentary about siblings affected by disabilities, several groups of brothers and sisters were interviewed. One of these families has five children—a set of triplets and two brothers with significant physical needs. The triplet teenagers help their two brothers by fulfilling many caregiving tasks. Each day, these triplets rise early so they can get their brothers out of bed, cleaned, and dressed before they get ready for school themselves.[2]

Oftentimes, children with disabilities have complicated health-related needs and histories—such as seizures, feeding tubes, or surgeries—that can affect the entire family. Elementary-age children learn about medical terminologies and often are faced with explaining their sibling's disabilities to others. Some even know how to administer special medications to their sibling, such as an EpiPen. If this is the case for your family, it's important that your children continue to see themselves—and interact with their disabled brother or sister— first and foremost as a *sibling* and not as a primary caregiver. If they are feeling frustrated or pressured in their

---

Watch this interesting and practical video about siblings: www.attitudelive.com/watch /brothers-and-sisters.
Do any of the stories resonate with you?
Are any of these experiences similar to those of your own children?

---

relationships with their sibling, they need to be able to discuss this with you, their parent, or another trusted adult.

Shandra tapped her foot as she waited outside the bathroom for her twelve-year-old sister to call her back in. Due to cerebral palsy, Latisha always needed help with toileting and other physical tasks. For years, Shandra had transferred her younger sister in and out of her wheelchair and also helped her at mealtimes. Though she didn't mind most of the time, she was often tired and frustrated. Everything with Latisha took so much time. Dinner usually lasted an hour because Latisha was a slow eater, and this cut into Shandra's time for homework and activities with friends. Shandra tried not to compare herself with her carefree friends who spent weekends at sleepovers or the mall, but sometimes this was difficult.

If your child feels this way, try not to be too hard on her. Every sibling deserves time to simply hang out with a brother or sister free from caregiving demands.

Many families qualify for state funding for respite care workers.[3] These workers are trained caregivers who are paid to care for children with disabilities so families can have some much-needed rest.

Additionally, Joni and Friends offers Family Retreats[4] nationwide throughout the year. If your family has never attended a Joni and Friends Family Retreat, consider taking your family to the next available one in your area. Every member of the family would enjoy making fun memories, as well as times of rest, relaxation, and receiving encouragement from other special-needs families.

Growing Up Together

Without a doubt, the demands of caring for a child or adult with special needs can be a heavy burden for the whole family, including your other children. But it's important for them to keep in mind that it's also tough on their brother or sister with a disability. Many children with disabilities miss out on enjoying everyday activities that most young people take for granted. No one enjoys taking medication or having multiple therapy or medical appointments. Encourage your nondisabled children to consider that their disabled sibling may feel guilt over how his or her needs limit the family's finances and time.

Chances are that all of your children may feel like they've been forced to grow up too fast. The question is, What can be done about it? It's a difficult situation, but you can help ensure your children relate to each other and feel valued.

For example, despite your best intentions, you may not always be able to attend your other children's sports or school activities as a result of having to take care of your child with special needs. This can be very disappointing for them. While you should attend whenever possible, it's not always feasible. In those cases, see if there are grandparents, aunts, uncles, or friends who could attend and cheer for your son or daughter. Ask them to take photos or videos of the event so you can share in the moment and celebrate with your child later on. When done with sincerity, this can communicate to your child that you really do want to spend time with him and that you're genuinely interested in what's going on in his life.

If your "typical" child is old enough to work, consider allowing her to get a part-time job so she can earn her own money. The goal is to reinforce that her activities and entertainment options are not being primarily dictated by her sibling's needs or preferences.

Lily, whose older sister has profound physical and intellectual disabilities, shares how this was her family's experience.

Growing up, I never really knew what types of music were popular. That is because my older sister, Sofia, almost always wanted to listen to *The Lion King* songs. It seemed like every day at home, I heard this music playing in the background, sometimes for hours on end. It was the only music that helped to calm Sofia when she was upset about something. She never outgrew her love for listening to *The Lion King*, but I eventually found private time to listen to music I enjoyed.

Sometimes children with disabilities have difficulty adapting to certain environments, which can affect their brothers and sisters as well. For example, children with intellectual, developmental, or behavioral disabilities may find it hard to wait for any length of time, thus limiting the activities that their families can enjoy together. Dining at sit-down restaurants or waiting in lines at amusement parks may be out of the question for children with certain disabilities, and so their families may avoid doing these things.

When nondisabled siblings realize that the types of fun things they can do as a family are limited, they may become bitter or annoyed. In these situations, it is especially important that families find pastimes they can share. Anna, a sibling whose older brother has intellectual and developmental disabilities, tells how her family found activities they could all enjoy.

Throughout my childhood and teenage years, my family never ate in sit-down restaurants because my brother simply could not wait. So we adapted by eating at buffet restaurants. Also, there were a lot of things that my older brother was not interested in doing—sports, arts, games. But he really liked to go boating and swimming, so every summer our family spent lots of time in the water! These times boating are some of my most precious memories of my family doing things together.

Are there certain things your children enjoy doing together? Consider how you as a parent can help facilitate those activities.

Growing Weary of Social Stigmas

Santiago drew back his hand and punched his classmate—hard. As the recess teacher pried Santiago away from his classmate, Santiago yelled at the top of his lungs, "You better take that back, or I'll hit you again. My brother is not a retard!" As the teacher led him toward the principal's office, Santiago blinked back tears. He was so mad at his classmate for making fun of his brother, Agustín, just because he had Down syndrome. Santiago often heard people making jokes about people with disabilities—on the bus, on the playground, at lunch—and each time it hurt his feelings. Today, though, when his classmate called Agustín a retard, Santiago could not just stand by without defending his brother. *Will things ever change?* Santiago wondered. *Will my friends ever stop looking down on people with disabilities?*

Santiago's struggles with other people's lack of empathy toward his brother are common. Soeren Palumbo, who has a younger sister with an intellectual disability, addressed the Illinois Senate a few years ago while he was in high school. In his compelling speech, he explained the frustration he felt when his peers made fun of people with disabilities and reflected on how having a sibling with disabilities positively influenced his life.[5]

Watch Soeren's six-minute speech at
www.youtube.com/watch?v=b9ut2feg2GU.
Are there similarities between Soeren's
experiences and those of your children?

Soeren's passion for defending his sister, and his increased awareness of the dignity of all people, are characteristics that many siblings of people with disabilities share. Unfortunately, this increased awareness, combined with the protective instincts we naturally feel toward our family members, can sometimes lead to painful social situations. Rosemary, a sibling of a brother with intellectual and developmental disabilities, recalls one of the most unpleasant interactions she had in high school.

When I was a high school junior, I took a psychology class. One day, the topic was mental retardation. Some of my outspoken classmates began making jokes about people with mental retardation, even comparing them to squirrels. Another classmate questioned what the purpose of people with mental retardation was, since she believed they could not achieve anything. Upon hearing these comments, I burst into tears; this was just so hurtful to hear! The teacher realized that I was upset, and she asked me if I had anything to say to my classmates. I responded by stating that my older brother had disabilities, that he was definitely not a squirrel, and that he was more of a person than my classmates. I then ran out of the classroom to compose myself.

Does your child find himself in similar circumstances? If so, it's crucial that he have the social support and encouragement he needs to help him deal constructively with those situations:

- You can offer a listening and understanding ear for him to vent his frustrations.
- Friends and classmates can be supportive by spending time hanging out or enjoying mutual hobbies or interests. Joining a club can be extremely helpful.
- Most important, he can find encouragement in his faith in Christ.

Growing Closer to God

Amid the challenges of being a family affected by disability, there is hope! God's Word is filled with beautiful promises that highlight how much He cares for and pays attention to us. Psalm 56:8 says that God keeps track of all our hurts, and He has even kept all our tears in a bottle and recorded them in a book. In fact, the Bible is filled with passages that show that God is personally concerned about and intimately aware of even the slightest details about our lives. For example, God knows the number of hairs on our heads,[6] and He specifically designed each of us in our mother's wombs.[7]

One of the psalmists wrote a powerful hymn from the depths of discouragement. Psalm 42 opens with the author graphically outlining his hurt—his enemies were jeering and mocking him, his tears were free flowing, and he was heartbroken. Despite the psalmist's distress, he knows that by focusing on God, he will find encouragement. Upon self-reflection, he states, "Why am I discouraged? Why is my heart so sad? I will put my hope in God! I will praise him again—my Savior and my God! Now I am deeply discouraged, but I will remember you [God]" (verses 5-6).

Think about all the times you have been sad or frustrated—or even cried because of your family's situation.

How might your nondisabled child's experiences be similar or different?

What does knowing that God has kept track of every time you have cried mean to you?

Note how his sorrow was transformed when he put his hope in God. This psalm has application for your entire family, including your nondisabled children. When they're feeling discouraged, it's important for them to put their hope in God, not in the things of this world. While family situations may disappoint, God never will.

You can also remind them that in heaven there will be

no more sadness or tears. In fact, God declares in Revelation 21:3-4 that He will live among His people, that He "will wipe every tear from their eyes, and there will be no more death or sorrow or crying or pain. All these things are gone forever."

Growing toward God's Calling

Many siblings choose careers in helping fields or fields where they work directly with people with disabilities.[8] Some believe that their experiences growing up with a brother or sister with disabilities prepared them uniquely to work in these fields. This was true for Shandra, who pursued a career in human services and has worked in nursing homes and group homes for many years. Her time spent caring for her sister while growing up helps Shandra to be more compassionate toward the clients with whom she now works. As an adult, Shandra is thankful for the many experiences she had with Latisha—even those that were challenging.

Jessica, likewise, credits a lifetime of watching her brother bravely endure multiple sclerosis for her passion to serve others and pursue a degree in physical therapy. She is grateful for the ways that God revealed Himself through her brother's weakness. Even though life was challenging at times, Jessica saw how God used their family's faithfulness to inspire others.

Encourage your "typical" child to consider the following questions:

- Is there something you have learned by helping your sibling with disabilities?
- How do you think this skill or lesson will influence your life in years to come?

While not all siblings affected by disabilities choose to enter healthcare or caregiving fields, many of them recognize positive influences from growing up with brothers or sisters with disabilities. Often they point out that they learned how to be responsible and levelheaded. Marie, an adult sibling of two brothers with multiple disabilities, explains:

> Growing up, I was often responsible for helping take care of my older brother, Steven. For example, if we had new babysitters, I showed them where everything was located in the house. When my younger brother, Danny, struggled with mental illness, I learned how to remain calm in all situations. At the time, I did not realize how these experiences shaped my personality, but once I left for college, people constantly commented on how calm and mature I was. I attribute these characteristics to my experiences with Steve and Danny.

As Marie's story demonstrates, the extra responsibilities that many siblings of persons with disabilities bear often develop into beneficial personality traits.

While it may be difficult for your child to recognize at this point, God has specific purposes for her. In Jeremiah 29, God tells the prophet Jeremiah to encourage the people of Judah who had been carried into exile from Jerusalem to Babylon. Despite this defeat by their enemies, God told His people that He had good plans for them, plans that included the nation's eventual restoration to their homeland.

Just as God had good and perfect plans for Judah, so He has perfect plans for each of us. When we think that our family situation is overwhelming and we are discouraged, we need to remember God's promises! As we saw in Joseph's story in chapter 9, God often uses difficult situations to refine a person's character and benefit many people. *All* of our children need to understand that God moves and works through our circumstances, and nothing happens to us that isn't part of His bigger plan.

Faith-Building for Siblings

While your children's situations as "typical" siblings affected by disabilities may seem discouraging at times, they can still remain thankful to God. Here are a few practical suggestions you can pass on to them to build up their faith.

- List things you are thankful for (big and small, silly or serious). For example, your list could include having a warm bed to sleep in at night, your favorite foods, or a talent you have. Thank God for each thing on your list.

- Ask God to teach you how to be thankful for your sibling with disabilities and unique family situation. You could pray something like this: "God, right now I am not at all thankful for my sibling. In fact, many times I am downright annoyed at how his (or her) disability affects my life. But your Word asks me to give thanks for everything. Please teach me how I can be thankful for my sibling and family."

11

Improving Communication

Seven-year-old Pranav blinked hard to hold back his tears and frustration. His five-year-old brother, Vihaan, was still not talking, which made it hard to play with him. When Pranav asked what game they should play, Vihaan just kept shaking his head no in response to every suggestion.

Because of his disabilities, Vihaan also had limited use of his arms and legs, so there weren't many activities these brothers could enjoy together. Why can't Vihaan talk like other kids? *Pranav wondered.* Why does everything have to be so hard for him?

PRANAV'S EXPERIENCE of trying to play with his brother is heartbreaking. It is an all-too-common experience, however, for siblings who have a brother or sister with speech impediments. Sometimes they can feel like they're having a one-sided conversation, especially if a sibling is nonverbal like Vihaan.

Communication problems can affect nondisabled siblings in more than one way. Many wrestle with complicated feelings of guilt, embarrassment, and frustration—to name just a few—but keep these emotions to themselves. That's why it's important for them to learn how to express their feelings to "safe" people who can help them.

Parents and others can help their children find creative ways to minimize frustration, increase communication, and share their feelings. Improving communication between siblings can strengthen bonds and create empathy, while expressing feelings can help nondisabled siblings learn they are not alone. Growing up in a family affected by disabilities is not always easy, but it often yields rich rewards in courage and character.

"Charlie can pinch, blurt out things, cry, laugh loud, jump, wrestle, and try my patience! Although I wish he could stop, he has still been a good influence on me. I love my brother even with his autism."

Maria, age 15

The Power of Communication

Pranav, now eight years old, smiled at Vihaan as they talked. Vihaan had recently received a specialized computer with a communication program that Vihaan activated with his eyes. Pranav was so excited to finally get to hear his brother answer his questions. For years, Pranav had often been frustrated because he didn't know what his brother was trying to communicate. This new computer was opening a whole new world of possibilities, and Pranav was thrilled.

Pranav's excitement over his brother's new speech computer is a great example of the power of communication. For siblings of people with disabilities, improved communication can be a pathway to a deeper sense of empathy. The ability to understand and share someone else's feelings is a skill that often takes years to develop. But as your children make the effort required to connect with their special-needs sibling, they'll likely find themselves becoming more empathetic toward their brother or sister and others as well, regardless of their abilities or weaknesses. Before Vihaan received his communication device, Pranav relied on Vihaan's gestures and responses to yes or no questions, which increased Pranav's patience and empathy.

Communication Takes Time

Fifteen-year-old Allison smiled as she listened to Roger's repetitive speech. As a result of his autism, Roger often asked the same questions over and over, and he had a narrow range of topics that he liked to talk about. He rarely asked her questions about how she was doing; his questions were always about his favorite things, such as going grocery shopping and eating dinner. Sometimes she found herself losing patience listening to the same questions and topics, but she had learned to interject teasing into their back-and-forth banter by giving a goofy answer to one of Roger's questions. Roger usually responded to Allison's teasing by correcting her and telling her the "right" answer, which caused them both to laugh.

Both Allison and Pranav faced unique challenges when it came to communicating with their sibling with disabilities. If you have a child with a speech-language disability, your other children may find themselves struggling to connect with this brother or sister. In these situations, be ready with some practical ideas about how they can best communicate with him or her. If your special-needs child is in school and receiving speech-language services, the teacher may have some ideas or suggestions for how to communicate more effectively.

Siblings may need a creative method to interact with their brother or sister, such as picture cards, sign language, or digital devices. Body language and technology are also avenues for improving sibling communication. Even individuals who physically cannot speak often can express themselves through nonverbal behaviors. For example, children who are unable to talk can simply shake their heads yes or no, or use a signal such as looking in one direction for yes and the other direction for no. Communication devices are available that allow individuals to type a response with their fingers or with eye-gaze tracking. Others may prefer to express their needs and wants by using an iPad app with picture cards or sign language, even if they are not deaf or hard of hearing.

When your children know the best way to communicate with their sibling, they can advocate for their brother or sister by teaching other people how to interact with him or her.

> "Growing up, our family never got to do normal things like going out to dinner, ball games, or movies. We always had to worry about how loud my brother got and what he would say."
>
> **Joshua, a computer engineer**

Encourage your children to discuss their sibling's communication style with friends in your church and neighborhood. They can help others feel comfortable using signs, picture cards, or a communication device. In doing so, they can play a powerful role in facilitating their brother's or sister's opportunities to connect with other people. This can also reduce a "typical" sibling's embarrassment or anxiety because friends will know what to expect.

Expressing Feelings

Hiroaki, now fourteen years old, sighed as he entered his guidance counselor's office. Mr. Green knew that Hiroaki's older brother, Kanaye, was hospitalized again for depression and wanted to make sure Hiroaki was okay.

Gritting his teeth, Hiroaki was determined not to tell Mr. Green how upset and worried he was about Kanaye. Admitting that Kanaye was in a difficult situation and that their family was struggling would surely bring shame and embarrassment upon his family—something that Hiroaki most definitely didn't want to do. Though he desperately wanted to talk with Mr. Green about his fears, Hiroaki just couldn't let his family down.

> "Due to my sister's autism, other kids made fun of her . . . and me. I love my sister, but it has been painful to watch her continuously repeat something that no one understands."
>
> **Heather, age 17**

Hiroaki's silence about his family's situation was eating him alive. His unvoiced heartache weighed him down and put a barrier between him and other people—people who wanted to help him.

Unfortunately, Hiroaki's hesitancy to share about his brother's disability is a common experience. Many children feel ashamed or embarrassed because of their sibling's disability, and it can be difficult for them to put these feelings into words. Children can also be embarrassed if their special-needs sibling does or says something inappropriate in public or in front of friends, such as commenting loudly on a stranger's appearance. They can also be frustrated and exhausted by their attempts to communicate with their sibling and feel as if no one understands their challenges.

In addition, nondisabled siblings may struggle knowing whom they can trust with their deepest feelings. Should they tell a close friend? Their grandparent? Aunt? Neighbor? Teacher? And if they do confide in someone, will that person even understand or relate to them? Would talking to others outside the family be disloyal to their sibling or parents?

It's natural for these children to experience confusing feelings and conflicting emotions. They may find it difficult to talk with their parents or family members who have their own issues related to their sibling's disabilities.

However, your nondisabled children's needs and problems are important regardless of the pressing needs of their sibling. Research shows that it is vital for siblings of children with disabilities to be able to express their needs and receive support. In fact, when steps are taken to ensure they stay emotionally healthy, the whole family benefits.[1]

Your child's reluctance to tell you or other trusted people about his feelings may be due to unhelpful advice that others have given him. For example, sometimes well-meaning adults tell young people that they need to be well behaved because their parents "have their hands full" with the needs of their child with disabilities.

This was the experience of Alicia Arenas, an adult sibling of two brothers with disabilities. A few years ago, Alicia gave a speech about her experiences as a sibling affected by disabilities. In her speech, Alicia defines this type of sibling as a "Glass Child," or a child whose needs are often overlooked by his or her parents because of the pressing needs of their child with a disability. To overcome the "Glass Child" syndrome, Alicia suggests that parents connect their nondisabled children with support groups or counseling and spend one-on-one time with them so they also feel special.[2]

As a parent, you need to initiate that one-on-one time. It is never too late to work on unresolved issues together. Consider what activities you could do together, such as taking a walk in the park or going out to lunch or for ice cream. If you have a hobby, sport, or other shared interest, consider doing that activity together. It may be hard with busy schedules, but it's important.[3]

Communication Outlets

Some siblings may find it difficult to share their feelings with their parents about their brother or sister with special needs. For example, children who are feeling particularly frustrated or upset may fear their parents' reactions. They might worry about being scolded or told that their feelings are wrong. If this is true in your family, you may need to help your children find other adults or friends in whom they can confide. As you do so, make sure you also reassure your children that you are always willing to listen.

You might suggest confiding in a close friend, mentor, teacher, or other trusted adult. If your "typical" children are in school, a guidance counselor or school social worker could offer a listening ear. Additionally, they may find it helpful to connect with other siblings affected by disabilities through online resources, such as blogs, Facebook pages, or the Sibling Leadership Network's website.[4] Tell your children that they are not alone; there are other siblings who have similar experiences. By plugging in to sibling support groups, they may develop deep friendships that will provide them with help and encouragement.

Find out if there is a Sibshop near you.[5] Sibshops are meetings designed for siblings of children with disabilities. These meetings usually are for elementary and middle school children, but there are a growing number of resources for younger and older siblings as well.

If these sorts of groups don't already exist in your area, consider helping your child start a sibling group in your church or community. The group could hold monthly meetings with games, food, music, crafts, Bible reading, and prayer time. Here are some helpful topics for discussion:

- How to Build Friendships
- How to Manage Anger
- How to Accept Differences
- How to Handle Frustrated Parents
- How to Cope with Jealousy
- How to Trust God in Loss

Some siblings find it helpful to write down the emotions they experience in response to their sibling's disabilities. Others enjoy writing stories or playing music, which helps them cope with the difficulties they face. Some are talented artists and find that creating something with their hands is a great emotional outlet. Physical activities, such as playing sports, swimming, or biking with friends, can relieve stress. Whatever the activity, the important thing is that your "typical" children find healthy, productive ways of processing the unique experiences they're going through. Your job as a parent is to help them find those outlets.

Building Connections, Finding Hope

Hiroaki smiled as he left Mr. Green's office. He felt like a ton of bricks had just been lifted off of his back. The night before, Hiroaki had learned that Kanaye would have to stay an additional month in the rehabilitation facility. Hiroaki was crushed; he had been hoping that his older brother would be home in time for his own upcoming fifteenth birthday dinner. Learning this news had

"My sister, Maggie, is my only sibling. At six months old she lost a third of her brain function. I miss having someone to share memories with, but we often look through family pictures. I tell her stories about our past adventures, and she laughs the whole time."

Sarah, a college senior

been the final straw; Hiroaki had decided to make an appointment to talk with Mr. Green, and he was so glad he did. Mr. Green had been very understanding and had given him information about local sibling support groups. Hiroaki couldn't wait to look up the websites! For the first time in months, he felt hopeful.

Learning to successfully communicate with a brother or sister affected by disabilities takes time and is not always easy. While communication challenges can teach children much about how to have patience and empathy, they may also bring to light some unconventional needs that require special supports from parents and friends. It is important that you find ways to help your nondisabled children connect with others, both within and outside your family, and receive the support they need to stay emotionally and spiritually healthy.

Above all, as your children struggle to learn how to communicate with their special-needs sibling and how to communicate their needs to others, they need to know that they are not alone.

You can begin a conversation with your "typical" children by sharing the next section with them—"What to Do When Things Are Difficult."

What to Do When Things Are Difficult

Have you ever felt frustrated by your sibling who has a disability? Have you ever felt embarrassed about your sibling? When hard things happen and you feel this way, you can ask God and others for help. Try these ideas:

- Take a few deep breaths. Then pray right away, no matter where you are. God wants you to ask Him for help when life is difficult. Psalm 145:18 says that the Lord "is close to all who call on him."

- Talk to your parents, a counselor, or someone else. Just make sure you feel safe sharing your thoughts with the person you choose. Someone else may have ideas that can help you in the future.

- Ask God to give you more patience and love for your sibling with disabilities. He can do it! Jesus Christ wants us to treat each other with compassion, kindness, humility, gentleness, and patience (Colossians 3:12-13). After all, that's how He treats us. It's not always easy to do, but God can help.

- Ask God to help you display the fruit of His Holy Spirit—love, joy, peace, patience, kindness, goodness, faithfulness, gentleness, and self-control (Galatians 5:22-23). Is there a fruit that is difficult for you to show others? You could make yourself a reminder bracelet, spelling out that fruit in lettered beads, or you could write the fruit on a small rock that you keep in your pocket. Touching or seeing a bracelet, rock, or other reminder can help you remember to think and pray.

Helpful Websites

Joni and Friends "Kids' Corner":
www.joniandfriends.org/kids-corner
Sibling Support Project:
www.siblingsupport.org
Sibling Leadership Network:
www.siblingleadership.org

12

Helping Siblings Connect

Shandra sighed heavily as she ended a call with a friend who had invited her to dinner. Shandra wanted to hang out with other teens more than anything, but she often had to decline. Tonight her parents were working late, and she was responsible for her younger sister, Latisha, who had cerebral palsy and couldn't feed herself or take care of her own physical needs.

As Shandra returned to the dinner table to continue feeding Latisha, her mind began to daydream about next year when she would move away to attend college. As far as she was concerned, that time couldn't come quickly enough. She would miss her sister but not the constant responsibilities and duties she'd had for so long.

❦

SHANDRA'S EXPERIENCE of caring for her sibling with physical disabilities is common. The responsibilities of feeding, toileting, and dressing those who can't do these things for themselves can make it difficult for young people to have time or energy to spend with their peers. But in daydreaming and wishing her life were different, Shandra is also missing out on the opportunities she now has to connect with her sister while they're still living under the same roof.

Fortunately, many siblings have discovered ways to enjoy

life with a brother or sister with a disability and even to strengthen their relationship before leaving home for college or a career. In this chapter, we'll take a look at the importance of connection among siblings and explore some practical ways in which connections between them can be facilitated. As you'll see, in your role as a parent you can be instrumental in helping your children develop connections that will last a lifetime.

Finding Common Ground

Allison, now thirty, smiled at her older brother with autism, Roger, as he sang and danced to his favorite Disney songs. Twenty years ago, the sound of those overly familiar songs had been so irritating. In time, she had learned to enjoy the things that Roger enjoyed, such as his Disney music and going grocery shopping. Once Allison could drive, she and Roger began taking trips into town to buy some of his favorite grocery items or to walk in the park. Her scrapbook was now filled with pictures of many of these minitrips. She thanked God for helping her learn to love and enjoy the times she spent with her older brother.

Research shows that children enjoy participating in activities with their siblings who have disabilities.[1] Yet young people find it difficult to connect with their brothers or sisters with special needs because of different interests or abilities. Lily, an adult sibling of an older sister with profound intellectual and physical disabilities, explains it this way:

When we were younger, I actually found it easier to connect with my sister, Sofia, since we had similar interests. I used to bring my toys into Sofia's room to play, and we both liked the same cartoon programs. Now that we are adults, however, it is harder to relate to her. We no longer share the same interests, so I have to be creative to connect with Sofia. Usually, our visits involve sharing a meal (I help feed her) and going outside for a walk.

There are a variety of reasons why a sibling might have difficulty connecting with a brother or sister who has a disability. Teenagers and adults with intellectual disabilities may have interests similar to younger children, while others may not be able to engage in certain physical activities because of their disability. In these situations, it's especially important to look for common ground that can be shared.

What interests do your "typical" children share with their sibling who has a disability? How can you, as a parent, promote their enjoyment of these shared interests?

While Shandra and Latisha may be somewhat limited in the kinds of physical activities they can do together, they can connect over common interests, such as cosmetics and hairstyling, movies, and music. Since Shandra feels particularly burdened by her caregiving duties, it's important for her to have quality time with Latisha that doesn't involve caregiving. For example, perhaps one night per week or per month, Shandra and Latisha can have a special "girls' night" together, where they order takeout food and watch a "chick flick."

Their parents could support this by buying the takeout food for them and paying for the movie rental. (Asking Shandra to pay for the expenses for both her and Latisha may make Shandra feel obligated or even upset that she is spending her limited financial resources on her sister.) It also may be helpful if Shandra and Latisha take turns selecting the movie and foods each week, as having Latisha do all the selecting could make Shandra feel like the night is more about Latisha than about the two of them.

Celebrating Personal Milestones

Pranav couldn't figure out what all the fuss was about. His elementary-school-age younger brother, Vihaan, had just received a Special Olympics medal for participating in a bocce ball event. Pranav could throw much farther than Vihaan, but his parents never gave him special celebration meals when he made long throws at his baseball games. His parents had taken many pictures of Vihaan with his medal, and they were going out to dinner later that night to celebrate. What was the big deal? Why was playing bocce ball so important?

Recognizing and celebrating each other's achievements and personal milestones is an important way that families foster respect and goodwill toward one another. In families affected by disability, however, those milestones can differ significantly from one person to another, and they can come at very different times than is usual in most families. For "typical" siblings, this can pose some unique issues.

When Pranav compared his personal milestones with those of his younger brother, he found major differences.

His confusion was compounded by not understanding why Vihaan's achievement was so important to his parents.

Pranav's parents could have helped the situation by explaining his brother's disability and how it affected his muscles and abilities. Research shows that learning about a sibling's disabilities fosters better understanding, empathy, and patience.[2] By helping Pranav understand his brother's differences, his parents could better explain why this Special Olympics medal was an important accomplishment for Vihaan. His parents could encourage Pranav to do something special to acknowledge Vihaan's accomplishment, such as verbally praising him or doing something unique to show his support of his brother's achievement.

For "typical" siblings, it can be difficult to understand why their brother's or sister's milestones—such as walking, talking, or graduating from high school—may come at much later times than their own similar milestones, or why parents and extended family members seem to give their sibling extra attention for achieving seemingly small things. You can help your children understand these and other aspects of their sibling's disability that may be unclear.

As you make sure to also celebrate your nondisabled children's milestones and achievements, it's good to point out how loved and honored *they* feel at the time. You can remind them that God wants His people to love each other in this way, and that means celebrating the milestones of their special-needs sibling, no matter how small they seem. Romans 12:10 says, "Love each other with genuine affection, and take delight in honoring each other," and Romans 12:15 says to "be happy with those who are happy." Helping siblings celebrate each other's achievements is also a way to create memories and help them bond.

Sharing Special Moments

Santiago, now in his mid-twenties, proudly stood
next to his twin as they waited in the church. Santiago
was getting married, and he was delighted to have
Agustín as his best man. Santiago had enjoyed having
his brother by his side throughout the wedding
preparation and at the ceremony. As he waited for his
bride, Santiago thanked God for the memorable times
he had enjoyed with Agustín in the weeks leading up
to this special day.

While it's not always possible to include a sibling with a
disability in one's wedding party, there are other ways of including him or her in this meaningful milestone. Kat, an adult sibling of a younger brother with intellectual disabilities, recalls
how her family ingeniously included him in her wedding.

Since Jacob didn't have the patience to sit through
my wedding, we opted to have a special dinner with
him to celebrate the occasion. My mom rented a tux
for Jacob, and I wore my wedding dress. We took
lots of pictures as a family, and then we had a special
dinner. Thus, we were able to include my brother
in the wedding celebration in a way that he could
understand and enjoy.

Kat wisely recognized that trying to include her brother
as part of the traditional wedding celebration would not be
practical or enjoyable for anyone, so she created a celebration
tailored to her brother's needs. Because of her thoughtful
planning, Kat's wedding album is now filled with photos

from the wedding dinner that include Jacob, as well as photos from the actual wedding ceremony.

Can you find creative ways to help your children connect during the special occasions of life?

Creative Ways to Connect

Teenage Pranav parked the family van and then hopped out to open the lift for Vihaan. They had just finished at Special Olympics practice, where Vihaan was preparing for an upcoming meet and Pranav was volunteering. They were about to enter one of their favorite burger places to order burgers, fries, and of course, milkshakes. Afterward, the two brothers would head home to play their favorite video games. The brothers spent nearly every free moment playing their games or just hanging out together, and Pranav enjoyed these laughter-filled times with Vihaan.

Some siblings of children with physical disabilities must be more creative in finding activities to do together, as Pranav and Vihaan's story demonstrates. Eating burgers and playing video games together connected the brothers in a way that was emotionally satisfying for them. Years ago when Pranav's parents explained his brother's disabilities to him, he gained a better understanding of and empathy for Vihaan. This deeper appreciation of his brother's achievements prompted Pranav to volunteer at Special Olympics events. Through his time volunteering, Pranav decided that he wanted to major in physical therapy. He credits his brother's special health care needs as one of the reasons why he now wants to become a physical therapist.

Connecting with the Help of Friends

College freshman Hiroaki threw the basketball to Kanaye, who deftly tossed it into the hoop. Jack and Simon, Hiroaki's friends from the Sibling Leadership Network,[3] were worthy basketball opponents, but their skills were no match for the brothers. The four friends met several times each week at their university's recreational center to play basketball. Hiroaki immensely enjoyed these times with his brother and friends. He was especially thankful that, thanks to supportive Christian friends, regular therapy, and medications, Kanaye's mental health had been stable for the past few years. Hiroaki sent a prayer of thanks to God for Kanaye's stability and for the friends whose encouragement had been invaluable over the years.

For Hiroaki, one of the major turning points in his relationship with his older brother occurred when he met other siblings affected by disabilities. Through getting involved at the Sibling Leadership Network, Hiroaki met Jack and Simon, who both had siblings with mental illness. These three friends offered invaluable support to one another, and they often gave each other ideas about how to connect with their siblings. It was Jack who had first suggested to Hiroaki that he find a sport to play with Kanaye, and this suggestion led to countless basketball games in the subsequent years.

The Power of Time

Shandra laughed at her sister's joke as they enjoyed a Saturday luncheon together, a tradition they had enjoyed for the past few years. Shandra, a recent college graduate and now a registered nurse, had chosen her career field because of her experiences of providing care for Latisha. While she used to feel bothered by caregiving, her feelings had changed when their parents started treating the sisters to a weekly girls' night while they were in high school. On those nights, their parents allowed them to order takeout from any restaurant and rent any movie they wanted. These nights were a catalyst for the girls' becoming close friends, and Shandra was thankful to her parents for encouraging these special times.

Shandra and Latisha's parents had wisely recognized that Shandra needed time with Latisha that was free from caregiving demands, so they provided a way for the sisters to relate. Through finding common ground, their friendship grew into a bond that extended past their high school years. Even when the girls moved to different homes, they continued to meet because they genuinely enjoyed spending time together.

The Hard Work of Connecting

As these vignettes illustrate, bonding with one's sibling is rarely easy, but it is worth it! The siblings in these chapters all agree that growing up alongside their brothers and sisters with disabilities has enriched their lives and refined their character. Allison and Santiago are quick to point out that their brothers taught them how to be patient, and Shandra gives her sister credit for teaching her how to be more compassionate.

A noteworthy similarity in these siblings' stories is that

when they were younger, they often didn't realize the ways in which their brothers and sisters with disabilities were positively influencing their lives. In fact, sometimes their lives were very difficult. Many times, these siblings asked God why their lives were so hard or why their sibling had disabilities.

While God doesn't always answer our questions immediately, He does promise that one day His people will understand His purposes. As Paul says in 1 Corinthians 13:12, while alive on earth we can only see a small part of what God is doing, but we will understand God's ways when we are fully known in heaven.

Isaiah explains that God's ways and understanding are much better than man's. Isaiah 55:8-9 says, "'My thoughts are nothing like your thoughts,' says the LORD. 'And my ways are far beyond anything you could imagine. For just as the heavens are higher than the earth, so my ways are higher than your ways and my thoughts higher than your thoughts.'"

Final Thoughts

Hebrews 11 is often called the "hall of faith" chapter, as it highlights testimonies of many people in the Old Testament who remained faithful to God despite challenging circumstances. Hebrews 12 explains that these faithful witnesses serve as a reminder to believers that we should "run with endurance the race God has set before us" (verse 1). In the same way, God calls us to faithfully run the races (our unique family situations) that are before us. We must remember that we are not alone. Remind your child that there are millions of other siblings who are also affected by disabilities.

Your "typical" childen may wonder why they've experienced some of the things they have. They may also wonder why their sibling has faced tough medical conditions, surgeries, or other hardships. In these situations, you can teach them that God is in control and that He cares about our needs. First Peter 5:7 says, "Give all your worries and cares to God, for he cares about you."

Help your children bring to Jesus the things that worry them and that they wish they understood better. Take time to talk with them about their questions and needs, and pray about them together. Ask Jesus to send comfort and to help them see how He is working out these circumstances for His good purposes.[4] And thank God for His love, care, and attention for you and your whole family!

Better Communication for Siblings

Milestone Chart

- Help all of your children create and decorate charts of the important milestones in their lives.
- Keep all charts in a prominent place in your home.
- As children reach new milestones, help them record those achievements on their charts.
- Find creative ways for your whole family to celebrate and rejoice in every achievement.
- Model God's truths that we are all equal in His sight and He loves us unconditionally.

PART 4

A Grandparent's Compassion

13

My Grandchild Has a Disability— Now What?

Margret and Henry couldn't stop the tears as their son shared the news.

Only a few months earlier, their daughter-in-law, Shelly, had asked them to help in the kitchen. "Would you mind checking on what I have in the oven?" she asked with a twinkle in her eye. There on the oven rack was a small bun with a note attached: Roses are red, violets are blue; on June fifteenth your grandbaby is due. *Squeals rang through the house as everyone came running to see.*

Now, something was dreadfully wrong. "Our daughter has Apert syndrome," their son Matt announced. "The doctor says it is a genetic disorder—something about the fusion of skull bones, fingers, toes . . . and for our daughter, her elbows. We won't have a complete diagnosis for some time, and there could be other complications."

❦

GRANDPARENTS EXPERIENCE a double measure of pain in moments like these—sorrow over what their grandchild will face and the burdens their adult children will bear. As grandparents, we have high hopes for our children and grandchildren. We dream of seeing them excel in school and become successful in life. We look forward to building meaningful relationships with them as we watch them grow and mature into all that God has purposed for their lives.

But when a grandchild is born with a disability or acquires one later on, there are so many questions—some with answers that are hard to accept. Still others may never be answered in this life. It's natural to wonder, *Now what? Where do we go from here? We are not prepared for this.*

Processing the initial shock and understanding what it all means can be difficult. You stand at a crossroads, facing a choice as to how you will respond. You want to believe this is all part of God's eternal plan, but what does it entail? What will this precious child and her parents have to endure? How many doctors, hospitals, surgeries, and therapies will there be? What will be the emotional and spiritual toll?

Knowing where you can help—and when it's best to give your family some "space" to work things out by themselves—are important pieces of the puzzle you must fit together so you can be a conduit of blessing to your children and grandchildren. But where do you turn for guidance?

Understanding Your Child, the Parent

Bob West, the founder and director of the Need Project, is helping build healthy relationships by supporting families of children with special needs. In a recent Need Project podcast interview with Lon Adams, a licensed family and marriage counselor, Bob asked about the range of emotions families often experience when first learning of their child's disability.[1]

Lon explained that in these circumstances it's normal to feel emotions similar to experiencing a death in the family. Sorrow, shock, anger, and depression are all common emotions for both parents and grandparents. Additionally, doubt about God's goodness can lead family members to ask, "How could God let this happen to us?"

While every situation is unique, and not everyone will handle the news in the same way, a tidal wave of emotions can be expected. As a grandparent, you will undoubtedly grieve over what your adult child and his or her spouse will face. It can be a tough journey.

But amid all the trials, there can be the joy of that first smile, the sweetness of watching one's child resting in peaceful sleep, and the dawning hope of a new dream for that child. If you can bear in mind this complex mix of joy and sorrow that your grown son or daughter is likely experiencing, then you will be in a better position to understand the roller coaster ride taking place in their minds. Their family's joys—and yours—can be brought about by something as simple as medical tests coming back negative. Similarly, small setbacks can produce painful grief. These highs and lows are part of a parent's day-to-day existence.

Individuals often experience grief in a cyclical rather than linear manner. It is normal to weather parts of one cycle, only to have fresh challenges send the grieving person back to a stage he or she has already experienced. Many of the specific challenges you can expect your adult children to encounter are discussed in earlier chapters of this book.

For now, a crucial first step is to understand what your adult children are going through emotionally. Reassure them that their emotions are natural and that your shoulder is available if they need a good cry. While you don't know all they are going through, let them know you want to be as supportive as possible. Your simple encouragement and understanding can be like wind in their sails.

Your Own Emotions

Don't be surprised if you experience many of the same feelings as your adult child. Some emotions can be magnified by feelings of helplessness, which can become stronger when you can't be nearby to offer practical assistance. When information is limited, your mind may rush to imagine worst-case scenarios. Your heart will ache not only for your grandchild but also for your adult child's distress. Recognize that you cannot take the entire burden of these circumstances on yourself.

You, too, will need a support system. Protect time to spend with your spouse or a good friend who will listen to you. It can be helpful to connect with other grandparents experiencing similar issues. There may be someone at church or in your neighborhood who can encourage you from God's Word and pray with you. If you don't find a support system and some way to process your feelings, you will likely be ineffective in supporting your children and grandchildren.

Understanding a Diagnosis

When medical professionals settle on a diagnosis, too many parents and grandparents take it as the final word regarding their loved ones. Keep in mind that a medical diagnosis involves just as much art (which is to say, educated guesswork) as it does science. Yes, some disabilities can be diagnosed definitively—an extra or missing chromosome, for example, can be seen under a microscope. Doctors can be reasonably confident of the presence or absence of certain physical, genetic, or cognitive traits.

Many disabilities, however, are not defined by a test result or an easily discernible ultrasound image. For most children, disabilities are diagnosed through observation in conjunction with cognitive or physical ability–based tests. In the end, medical tests may show the presence of something or the absence of something else, but they never tell the whole story. Most important, they can't reveal who the person really *is*— only God knows that.

Consider a large extended family. Family members have many of the same genes, common ancestry, and similar traits. There may even be identical twins in the mix. Yet no one doubts the uniqueness of each person in the family tree. This is similarly true for people with any particular disability. Diagnoses may play a part in shaping your grandchild's future, but they will never wholly define who he or she will become. A doctor's long-term prognosis cannot describe your grandchild's future with total accuracy; it is not the final road map for your grandchild's life.

Yet in many instances, a medical diagnosis is valuable. Without it, access to doctors and therapists, as well as community and school resources, may not be available. Once a child has a medically confirmed diagnosis, the door to all kinds of services can often be unlocked.

Bob and Sue West know well how insufficient a diagnosis can be when it comes to predicting a child's future. Their son Kyle was born two months premature. When he was six months old, Kyle was referred to a specialist who gave the Wests a lengthy list of possible diagnoses. It wasn't until Kyle was two years old that he was diagnosed with cerebral palsy. Reading the definition of this disease and the full range of medical prognoses associated with it could have made the future look grim for Kyle.

In those confusing, stressful days of caring for a special-needs infant, Bob and Sue had no idea that Kyle would one day be working toward his master's degree at the University of

Colorado, Boulder. To be sure, Kyle faces ongoing struggles with the physical aspects of his disability. He has been through more than a dozen surgeries over his twenty-four years. And Kyle's story will not be the same as that of other children with cerebral palsy, some of whom will face greater difficulties—and some less—than Kyle. But Kyle's diagnosis is not who he is.

A diagnosis is not the final word on your grandchild's future either. All children are unique and precious, and God has a plan for each life.

Help Them Connect

As parents manage their child's disability, they may seem to be taking on another full-time job. There can be an endless stream of doctor's appointments, therapy sessions, and—depending on the child's health—multiple surgeries and hospital stays. This is often very difficult to coordinate.

If your grandchild has siblings, remember they also have emotional and physical needs that parents must meet, such as help with homework, advice for any problems, and rides to school and activities.

All of these responsibilities can cause families to live in survival mode. Your support can help the family avoid that and allow time for enjoyable activities.

Every family faces seasons of busyness and stress that make it essential to change priorities and manage time differently. Yet the demands of having a child with special needs can cause a family's stress levels to escalate. The family may become so focused on caring for one child that they no longer see the unique needs of other family members. Parents can run themselves ragged, which can aggravate or even cause personal health issues and put family relationships at risk.

Be a Safety Net

One relationship that frequently suffers, often disproportion-ately so, is the relationship between husband and wife. When couples don't take time to rest and connect with each other, they can find their marriage struggling. If their child's disability is profound, it may be nearly impossible to find suitable caregivers for even a brief date night.

> When a couple doesn't take time to rest and connect, their marriage can suffer.

As a grandparent, you can make a real difference in this area. Depending on how complicated the situation is, arranging time for your grown children to get away may require plenty of creativity, but it can be the perfect opportunity to foster better relationships.

What your family most needs from you is to be sensitive to their situation. It's vital that both extended family and friends actively embrace your grandchild's family with love and care, supporting them as each new need arises. If you are not sure where to start, here are a few ideas:

- Provide frozen meals for those days when no one has the energy to cook.
- Volunteer to watch your other grandchildren during medical appointments so that everyone doesn't have to sit in the doctor's office.
- Offer to care for your special-needs grandchild for a day or afternoon so Mom and Dad can be freed up to spend time with their other children or with each other.

Above all, remember that your grandchild's family will need your help not only during the first few weeks or months after a disability enters their daily lives—but they will also need your ongoing commitment and understanding for the long haul. Your family is running a marathon race, not a sprint. Many families find plenty of support from their community and church during the initial weeks of this challenge, but unfortunately, this support often dries up over time.

On the other hand, families struggling to meet need after need may grow weary of burdening everyone else with their problems. Your adult children may become reluctant to keep coming to you for help because they do not want to impose. The best remedy for this is to stay in close contact. Never be afraid to ask them what they need *today*. Continue to assure them that you want to help, even when everyone else returns to life as normal. Reiterate that they can call you when they need you most.

When you settle into a regular cycle of checking in or stopping by, you become the "safety net" that parents so desperately need. Regularly scheduled times together will let you observe how well they are doing so that you know when and how to offer help.

Advice and Comments

When you share the news that your grandchild has a disability, whether at church or with extended family or friends, many will not know what to say. It isn't that they have any ill intentions, or that they are insensitive or cruel. They may never have experienced something similar and don't know how to help you process what you're going through. They may, in fact, offer advice or comments that can be quite hurtful. Most people mean well, even if it doesn't seem so.

Bob and Sue West felt the sting of this soon after their son Kyle was first diagnosed with cerebral palsy. Bob's grandmother was a first-generation immigrant from Guatemala. As Bob and Sue sat with her at a family event, she grabbed Bob's hand and told him about something that had happened in her home country. She said that when Bob's cousin was young and not yet walking, his legs had been "fixed" by having egg whites rubbed on them. Bob was in no mood to hear of some "miracle cure." He angrily explained to his grandmother that egg whites were not going to cure his son's disability. It wasn't until much later that he understood that his grandmother was simply trying to help in the only way she knew how.

If you have not yet had people share how special therapies, diets, or vitamins cured someone with a condition similar to that of your grandchild, you likely will. While these may be appropriate means for mitigating the effects of your grandchild's disability, trust your adult children. The research-based knowledge they have gleaned from medical experts familiar with your grandchild's specific condition and other parents of children with similar needs almost always far exceeds the value of well-meaning but ill-informed advisers.

In addition to hearing of miracle cures from others, be prepared for distraught condolences that hurt more than they comfort. One grandmother shared that when her Bible study group found out about her newborn granddaughter's Down syndrome, she began receiving grief cards more suitable after a death in the family. The family had been rejoicing in the birth of their new little girl, and the cards hurt deeply.

The beginning of a new life, regardless of its challenges,

is never a tragedy. Even so, you will likely encounter people who are unsure how to react and, perhaps with the best of intentions, treat it as such.

Wisdom is required when giving and receiving input from others. The same is true when passing on information or advice to your adult children; be mindful that it may not be appropriate for the time and place. In some cases, it may be wiser not to share it at all, but instead to trust that they are doing their best for their child—your grandchild. Sometimes a silent, sincere hug speaks louder than words. James 1:19 provides a good reminder for us in this regard: "You must all be quick to listen, [and] slow to speak."

Above All Things, Pray

Even in the best of circumstances, issues and questions arise in our lives that are beyond our ability to understand. Our heavenly Father, however, has a perfect grasp of each situation. He is the ultimate Source of comfort, care, and strength. He knows each hair on your head, not to mention the head of your child and grandchild! He is not taken by surprise at the struggles you face. With complete confidence, you can trust all things to Him—all your fears and each of your needs. So "never stop praying" (1 Thessalonians 5:17)!

A Prayer Guide for Your Grandchildren

- *Pray for healing:* God can and does heal. It is often a mystery to us why some receive healing and some do not, because His purposes are beyond our understanding. Still, He always has compassion for those who are experiencing pain and suffering, and He tells us to pray for our grandchildren's health and wellness. *Psalm 30:2; James 5:13-15*

• *Pray for strength:* Ask God to give strength to your children and grandchildren so they can thrive despite the challenges they face. Pray that you will have strength to support them in meaningful ways. *Philippians 4:13; 1 Peter 4:11*

• *Pray for understanding:* While there are many common threads, a family's needs are unique in every case, and insight is crucial to determine where you can be most helpful. Ask God to give you keen insight as to your role. *Psalm 32:8; Proverbs 3:5-6*

• *Pray for grace:* Pray that your family would show grace for one another—husbands to wives and wives to husbands; parents to children and children to parents. Pray, too, that grandparents would display grace to their children and grandchildren (and vice versa). Stress can bring out the worst in all of us. Ask God to flood your family with His grace during difficult times when we're less than our best. *Matthew 6:14-15; Ephesians 4:29*

• *Pray for wisdom:* Ask God for wisdom for your children, grandchildren, and all the doctors and professionals who treat your grandchild. Pray for godly wisdom and unity on medical decisions affecting your grandchild's life. Pray that your adult children will see the needs of the entire family and make wise choices. *Ecclesiastes 7:12; James 1:5-8*

• *Pray for faith:* Pray that your family would know Jesus Christ as Savior and Lord and grow deeper in their relationship with Him. Pray they will know God, their Creator, as the Source of everything they need. Ask Him to guard your own heart so you can be a conduit of Christ's love and grace to each grandchild and their parents. *John 3:16; Hebrews 11:6; 1 John 1:9*

• *Pray the words of James 1:2-4:* Ask for the joy of the Lord for your family as you persevere in the midst of trials!

14
Supporting Your Grandchild

My grandson Max has autism. Learning to meet his needs has been one of my greatest challenges but also one of my greatest blessings. When Max comes to visit, everything else goes on hold, and I accommodate myself to his schedule and his needs. Spending time with him helps me focus on what truly matters in life.

In a utilitarian worldview, Max's life is meaningless. Why, then, does he bring so much joy to his family and friends? Max's autism is not a good thing—it's part of the world's brokenness—and yet that brokenness has been used to enlarge our capacity to love. Max brings joy into our lives through our sacrifices for him. Max himself knows a joy and wonder that puts me to shame. Looking at his life, I have to conclude that the good life is not about the sum total of what we contribute to the world. It's about loving.

THE LATE CHUCK COLSON—FOUNDER OF PRISON FELLOWSHIP
AND THE COLSON CENTER FOR CHRISTIAN WORLDVIEW

WHEN DORI WAS BORN, she was as beautiful and healthy as any other newborn. Within a few short weeks, however, she began experiencing some ongoing gastrointestinal issues. Her parents, Whitney and Lars, were alarmed. The doctor eventually ordered more blood tests for Dori, which indicated a metabolic disorder. After an appointment with a neurologist,

Whitney and Lars received the news that their daughter might have cerebral palsy in combination with microcephaly, a known cause of intellectual disabilities. More tests would be needed to know for certain.

Dori's parents and grandparents tried to process this shocking news. *What would it mean for Dori?* In God's sovereignty, they were drawn to a church prayer meeting that they'd never attended. During the service, the pastor felt strongly that someone needed specific prayer that night and invited the people to turn to someone nearby and share their prayer requests. Whitney felt so fragile that she didn't want to talk to complete strangers about her daughter. But before she knew what was happening, her mother had turned to a nearby couple and began telling them about Dori's condition. Whitney recalls the experience:

> As the pastor shared and we began to pray, I had time to reflect. I tried to appear strong, but inside I was falling apart because I didn't know what lay ahead. Tears rolled down my cheeks as a Jeremy Camp song, "Mighty to Save," began to play. Suddenly, a wave of peace came over me.
>
> "Savior, He can move the mountains; my God is mighty to save, He is mighty to save": The moment I began to sing, I felt that whatever the road ahead held for Dori and our family, it would be okay. Somehow, we would all be able to face the storm.

Dori's tests continued until a final diagnosis was reached. Throughout the long ordeal, they all remained hopeful and clung to God's promise in Isaiah 41:10: "Don't be afraid, for

I am with you. Don't be discouraged, for I am your God [and Dori's]. I will strengthen you and help you. I will hold you up with my victorious right hand."

At age four, Dori's condition was finally diagnosed as CASK-gene syndrome. Only around fifty cases of this syndrome are known of worldwide, and only girls survive it. There are numerous symptoms, including a small head circumference and cognitive disability.[1] Dori is nonverbal, but she did start walking at age four, which is almost unheard of for this disability.

How would you support a grandchild in this situation?

Ted and Deb, Dori's maternal grandparents, and Sandy, her paternal grandmother, discussed what kind of support they could provide given their precious granddaughter's disability. Together, they determined to do the best they could according to what God had given them. It was an intentional choice to be attentive to Dori's needs no matter what it cost them, as well as to the needs of her brother, Dylan, and her parents—their own children.

These are admirable and courageous attitudes, especially when they're put into practice. In Matthew 7:24-27, Jesus says a wise man puts into practice what he knows to be true, and as a result, his house will have a strong foundation. But what does it look like to care for a grandchild with a disability, one whom God has given us to love and value?

One thing is clear: Children with special needs and their parents deserve our understanding, even when they're reluctant to ask for it. More important, parents want to know that their family will be a source of intentional support and unconditional love for their children. Let's examine a few practical ways to do that.

Be Intentional

Grandparents Dave and Claudia are in a unique situation. Their two-year-old grandson, Sam, has severe disabilities associated with hydrocephalus and a seizure disorder, and Sam's father, their son Tim, has Parkinson's disease. This means they must intentionally give careful thought to how they can be present for both of them. Dave and Claudia have come to believe that they can best support their grandson by encouraging and affirming their son and daughter-in-law.

"We think it's important for our son and daughter-in-law to be able to enjoy personal time together," Dave explains. "Since they're Sam's primary caregivers, we make ourselves available by being 'on call' to help as needed."

These grandparents are intentionally striving to fulfill the apostle Paul's admonition to the church, which is the family of God. Galatians 6:2 says, "Carry each other's burdens, and in this way you will fulfill the law of Christ" (NIV). Though it's less common nowadays for multiple generations of a family to live together under the same roof, as was common in biblical times, this mandate still includes grandparents. Grandparents are in a unique position to help their adult children bear the physical and emotional burdens required to daily care for a child with disabilities. Even parents of children without disabilities need the experience and wisdom of loving, involved grandparents.

For some families, this level of closeness may not be the norm because of unresolved tensions. Yet it is never too late to build new relationships with your adult children. Regardless of what has happened in the past, consider the promises of God to restore your family.

In Old Testament times, God used a devastating locust

plague to turn the hearts of His people back to Him. Through the prophet Joel, God gave the Israelites this hope of restoration if they returned to Him: "The LORD says, 'I will give you back what you lost to the swarming locusts. . . . Once again you will have all the food you want, and you will praise the LORD your God, who does these miracles for you'" (Joel 2:25-26).

Just as He did with the people of Israel, God uses the "disasters" of our lives to break down our illusions of self-sufficiency and reveal the importance of our relationships with Him and others. In the end, God desires that all families be restored so they can support one another—and through His Spirit, He can make us agents of reconciliation even in the most difficult of family situations.[2]

As a grandparent of children with disabilities, you have the potential for being the most effective source of support in four key areas: emotional, relational, financial, and spiritual. In this chapter, we'll focus on the first three; we'll address the fourth in the next two chapters.

Emotional Support

Because we are made in the image of God, human beings experience a variety of emotions. This is especially true for your grandchild with a disability. Whether or not she is able to express her deepest feelings, her emotions are a vital part of who she is. And like all human beings, she deserves to know love, expressed through genuine affection, kindness, and joy.

You may not be financially rich, but you have a wealth of emotional stock to offer your grandchildren. They need your touch, your words of blessing, and your expressions of delight in them. This kind of emotional support makes them feel safe in your presence and cherished as gifts of God.

Speak to your grandchildren often about how precious and valued they are to you and to God. The psalmist declares, "Thank you for making me so wonderfully complex! Your workmanship is marvelous—how well I know it" (Psalm 139:14). Speak that truth over and over. Tell them how amazing and talented they are—how their smiles light up a room. Praise them for small signs of progress, affirming their worth to you and their families. Smile with your eyes when you are around them so they can see the authenticity of your delight in them. (For more suggestions, see "Prescription for Praise" at the end of this chapter.)

Ron and Cookie use two things in particular to emotionally engage their granddaughter, Samantha. Sam has Down syndrome and sometimes erupts in out-of-control tantrums. Ron and Cookie discovered that playing music calms her and focuses her attention on something that makes her smile and laugh. They also take her on rides in the car because there's almost nothing she enjoys more. It's a great way for them to connect and have fun together.

Many grandparents have discovered that singing songs and listening to music are great ways to connect emotionally with their grandchildren. For some children, hearing stories read aloud creates a warm and secure environment. There is something about the sound of a grandparent's voice that calms a child's spirit.

A great tool called LuvYa Reader (www.luvyareader .com) allows you to record your own voice reading Bible stories and age-appropriate devotionals. Once recorded, you can e-mail them to your grandchild so he can hear you tell the stories. It's great for grandparents who live miles away because it still allows them to be emotionally present.

Your adult children also need emotional support. One

single mother said, "I wish my parents knew how alone I feel and how much I need someone I can talk to about my fears and feelings. I realize that I can't live my life like typical parents do, but if they could help me escape the disability routine for just a few hours, it would mean so much."

When one father was asked about his parents' support for his family, he said, "My parents have been very supportive of our decision to keep and nurture our son, who has many physical challenges. Fortunately, they see him as a gift of God and tell us how much they pray for our family. But in the day-to-day reality, they are not involved. I wish they'd show more interest and be willing to interact with us more than by just dropping in on holidays."

It's your choice, Grandpa and Grandma. Don't be like the grandmother who said, "I didn't support my kids like I should have, because I thought they didn't need me." What makes this especially sad is that this grandmother never asked her daughter what she needed. Don't be afraid to ask—but if you do, be sure you are willing to follow through.

Relational Support

"Grandparents still have a call to *go after* their grandchild," one heartbroken parent declared. What does this mean? Grandparents need to make an extra effort to connect with their grandchild, which often means making some sacrifices—but not as many as Mom and Dad are already making! It will require some creative thinking and effort to be there for your grandchild. It also means not giving up. It might be hard, even discouraging at times, but keep trying.

You can't provide relational support if you don't know what your children and grandchildren need. You may have to ask in a few different ways before you fully understand your family's unique needs, but keep asking—and keep talking! Ask your children specifically about what would most help their children. It is likely that your children actually *want* to tell you, but their own pride might stop them. If so, assure them that they are precious to you and that God made all of you "family" for a reason: to love and care for one another.

Once your adult children see that you really want to help, they'll appreciate your genuine effort to connect with them. Start with helping your special-needs grandchild to feel comfortable around you. Parents must become confident in your ability to care for their child if they leave the house for a few hours to rest and regain some energy. Here are a few suggestions to help you understand what's needed:

- *Be familiar:* Your grandchild needs to see you often. If you live a long distance away, call or e-mail as often as you can. Learn to use Internet video chat technology; it's wonderful! Your voice and actions on video can reveal your love and deeply influence children.

- *Be available and flexible:* Things can change rapidly with a child who has disabilities. Be willing to adjust and respond quickly when required.

- *Be creative:* Your grandchild with special needs may not respond to the same things as your other grandchildren do. Look for imaginative ways to help them learn, grow, and express themselves.

- *Be a good listener:* If you want to know how best to relate to your grandchild, listen to the parents' advice. And sometimes your adult child simply wants to vent frustrations; in those instances, listen and don't feel compelled to offer solutions.

- *Be sure your viewpoint is holistic:* See your grandchild as God sees her. Look at the whole child, not just the disability. Help your grandchild discover the gifts and talents that God gave her for His purposes. Let her know how much you delight in her efforts.

Financial Support

Jon had to juggle all the balls as a newly divorced father in order to be an effective single dad: working a full-time job, guiding his son, addressing the needs of his daughter with Down syndrome, and finding another place to live.

Fortunately, Jon's parents had decided a few years earlier to move closer to Jon to help out with their granddaughter. They invited Jon and the kids to move in with them until he could find a house that would work for his family. With their financial assistance, Jon was able to secure a house close to Grandma and Grandpa. Without their help, this would have been very difficult, if not impossible. It provided Jennifer a home with her brother and father where she could flourish.

Depending on the family's circumstances and the severity of your grandchild's disability, financial burdens can significantly affect your children and grandchildren. According to one US study, 40 percent of families with "children with special health care needs" experience a "financial burden related to their child's condition."[3] When faced with major health issues, many families are forced to change their standard of living. Often one of the parents must quit a job and stay home to care for their child.

Good health insurance can be an indispensable blessing,

but there are almost always costs that aren't covered. Out-of-pocket expenditures can put a family in real financial trouble, even when they have insurance.

If your grandchild has ambulatory needs, purchasing a wheelchair-accessible van can be prohibitive for a family. If you're blessed with the resources to aid your family financially, you can provide incredible relief by addressing some of your loved ones' most basic needs. In addition to covering medical costs, you might consider providing airline travel, vacations, or extended breaks from their regular routines.

Amy, a military wife, describes how her parents have been an amazing source of support for her family: "Both our families spoil our children. They often watch them to give my husband and me much-needed breaks. Sometimes they pay for our children's birthday parties and camps. When my husband is deployed, my family picks us up, and we stay with them until he comes back."

While not all grandparents have ample fiscal resources, some are able to help carry the load. Even minimal support can make a big difference. Some other common kinds of support include mobility equipment, therapy sessions, home modifications, and personal needs. Such financial assistance can be valuable to the family's welfare. Whatever the level of your involvement, remember that you're assisting not only your adult children but also your grandchild.

A word of caution, particulary if you're contemplating transferring significant financial or other material assets to benefit your grandchild: Be careful to do so in a way that does not unnecessarily jeopardize the child's access to government or health benefits that may be important for his or her long-term well-being. A "special-needs trust" is often the best way to go in such cases.[4]

If your finances are limited and you're unable to offer major monetary support, your children will understand. Consider other ways you can help with your family's financial needs. A few examples follow:

- Organize a church or community fund-raiser to help cover a specific cost, like home remodeling (for greater accessibility) or reliable transportation. Check out online campaign sites such as GoFundMe, which have been very successful for aiding worthy causes. See www .gofundme.com.

- Research national grants and local organizations that support children and families affected by disabilities. You'll be surprised by the numerous resources and people who are willing to help families overcome pressing circumstances.

Remember that any support you offer your adult children has been provided to you by God and generously passed along to them by Christ Jesus. Your grandchild may not be able to identify what you are doing, but your gifts can reduce the stress felt by his parents and have a positive effect on everyone. Easing the financial burden can free up the family to address other stressful circumstances.

> Find the "Ultimate List of Grants and Resources for Families with Special Needs" at www .joyfuljourneymom.com/ultimate-list-of-grants -and-resources-for-families-with-special-needs.

The Best Investment

When Jesus told His disciples the parable of the talents, the issue was not the amount each servant was given, but what each did with it. God has entrusted resources—time, talent, and treasure—to each of us. The question the Master asks of us is this: "What did you do with what I gave you?"

Whether it's a matter of providing emotional, relational, spiritual, financial, or other forms of support, you have so much available to invest in the lives of your children and grandchildren. Put it to work!

Prescription for Praise

Awesome!
Clever!
Right on!
You made my day!
Keep at it!
High *five*!
You're on target!
Super effort!
You deserve a hug!

Find more ideas in "100+ Ways to Praise a Child," available at www.speechtherapygames.com/freebies /waystopraiseachild.pdf.

When you shower grandchildren with praise, you give them a glimpse of God's unconditional acceptance. Buried deep in the hearts of many special-needs children, however, is a contradictory message that says "You're not good enough." Words of praise have the power to build their self-esteem, shape attitudes, and help them reach attainable goals.

Praise needs to be real and genuine. Children might view false praise as a way to manipulate their behaviors. Here are some things to remember about praise:

- Children want you to notice their smallest attempts to help others: "Rosie, I like the way you shared your markers with Lynn."
- Praise comes in many forms. Grandchildren like to receive notes, phone calls, e-mails, text messages, small gifts, stickers, pictures, etc.
- Praise children for their actions and character rather than their appearance. Instead of saying, "Your hair looks nice," say things like "You were so kind to pick up that book for me."
- Thanking God for children in prayer is a form of praise: "I thank the Lord that _____ is in our family."

Notes of Praise for Grandchildren

(Simply copy, sign, and send.)

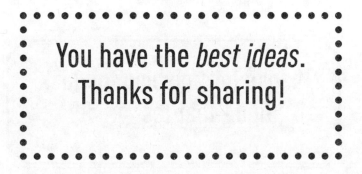

You have the *best ideas*.
Thanks for sharing!

You made a *good* choice today!
That made me *happy*!

You enjoy helping others.
That is just what Jesus would do!

Thanks for finishing the task.
Didn't that feel great?

15

Huge Investments, Huge Rewards

*"Grandparents have become the family safety net, and I don't see that
changing any time soon," said Amy Goyer, a family expert at AARP.
"While they will continue to enjoy their traditional roles, including
spending on gifts for grandchildren, I see them increasingly paying
for extras that parents are struggling to keep up with—sports, camps,
tutoring or other educational needs, such as music lessons." . . .*

*Currently about 5.8 million children, or nearly 8 percent of
all children, are living with grandparents identified as the head of
household, according to 50-state census data.*

"GRANDPARENTS PLAY A BIGGER ROLE IN CHILD-REARING," BY
HOPE YEN

❦

WHO DOESN'T LIKE showing off pictures of their grandchildren? And thanks to smartphones and iPads, we're not
limited by the number of photos we can stuff into a wal-
let. It's never been easier to corner friends or coworkers and
brag about our smart, talented, mischievous, and "cute-as-a-
button" grandkids. What a blessing to all!

Grandparents enjoy sharing stories about grandchildren,
and most can be counted on to repeat them—over and over!
The places you've been together, the toys you keep in your

home, the smells of certain foods you share together—all these things put a big smile on your face.

If you've had grandchildren for a while, you know that grandparenting challenges come along with the smiles, even in the best of circumstances. And having a grandchild with special needs is probably not what you ever envisioned for yourself. Yet if you keep an open heart and mind, this journey called "disability" can be filled with unexpected blessings and big rewards. The joy can be so vibrant that you find yourself overwhelmed by the goodness of God. Yes, the path can be messy and sometimes scary. You might be called on to do things that surprise you and make you uncomfortable. But as you hang on to the truth that God will supply all your needs,[1] you will discover a depth of love that you might never have experienced. Your investment in the life of your grandchild can reap huge dividends for your entire family.

When Joshua led the Israelites across the Jordan River, he instructed the priests to carry the Ark of the Covenant in front of the people. As a test of their faith, the priests had to step into the water first—only then did God part the river.[2] He wants to do the same for you and your family. Though He may test your faith, He is never unkind. And He always keeps His promises.

You can "step into the waters" in many ways. And as you invest in the life of the grandson or granddaughter God has given you, you'll also reap the rewards of His glorious goodness.

Investing in the Marriage

Grandparents Bruce and Patricia live in the same city as their daughter Melissa's family. The past few years have been challenging for Melissa and Tim, whose daughter Abigail has Down syndrome. From the time of their granddaughter's diagnosis onward, Bruce and Patricia have been heavily involved, as have Tim's parents, Richard and Peggy.

When Melissa had to stay in the hospital during her pregnancy, Patricia and Peggy traded off watching the older two children and took them to their activities and to visit Mom. Now that Abigail is older, they continue to watch all the kids when Tim and Melissa need time for appointments and activities. They often invite all the children for the weekend, providing respite for their own adult children.

"We feel it is healthy for their marriage and for us to get to know our grandchildren," Bruce said. "Sometimes Tim and Melissa live on little sleep for long periods of time and face a lot of stress. If a small thing like taking the kids for the weekend gives them a little break, we are happy to do it. We do wish we could do it more often."

Providing this kind of support is not always easy. Sometimes a grandchild's medical need arises at a moment's notice. Managing special care can be intimidating—even scary—for parents, let alone grandparents. It can require extra

Grandparents have incredible potential to influence the next generation, as well as a biblical mandate to do so. But sadly, they are generally overlooked, underresourced, mislabeled, and underappreciated. The Legacy Coalition believes it is time for grandparents to unite and chart a new course. To learn more about their national conferences and how to launch a grandparenting ministry in your church, visit www.legacycoalition.com.

effort and time to figure out what is actually needed. In some situations, everyone involved must be trained in administering a particular treatment.

Investing in your grandchild in this way, however, can go a long way toward helping your adult children have a healthier and happier relationship. When that happens, your grandchild will enjoy the benefits of a stable family. Your efforts will produce fruit in your family for generations and leave a lasting legacy.

Investing in the Child

To outsiders, many parents of children with special needs appear to be "superparents" who have it all together. It's as if God has given them some extraordinary strength and knowledge for this task. While we know God supplies what we need to face life's challenges, these parents readily admit that they are ordinary people doing what is necessary for their child. And no, they don't have all the answers.

Fear can be a big factor for parents of a child with disabilities, especially if things have not gone well in the past. If they have always been the ones to do everything for their child, they can feel uncomfortable and even vulnerable when letting others help—even grandparents. New situations can be risky for a fragile child, which makes it harder for parents to trust other people, even when their offers of help are clearly made with the best intentions.

As a grandparent, you may have to work at building trust with your grandchild's parents—for the benefit of your grandchild. Persistently "lean into" your adult children and don't give up, even if they insist there is nothing you can do. Stay involved as much as you're permitted to be, and prayerfully trust God to direct you and your children.

Bob West remembers how his mother-in-law took this step for his family. When Bob's son Kyle was a toddler, he was unable to walk like the other children in Sunday school class. He was learning to use a walker to get around, but they were fearful of leaving him in class with all the rambunctious and uncoordinated toddlers. Bob's fear was that the other children would run into Kyle and trample him.

His mother-in-law offered to help in a small but critical way. She stepped in and told him that if he brought Kyle to the earlier service, she would stay with him in the class while Bob and his wife went to church. So every week, with few exceptions, she showed up to be with him and give her family the peace of knowing that someone who cared was watching out for Kyle.

When it came time for Kyle to attend college sixteen hundred miles away, Dad was uneasy about letting him take that risk. Yet he was able to let go because Kyle's grandmother had invested in her grandson all those years ago. What a powerful difference the sacrifice of her Sunday mornings made in Kyle's future.

Mark often brags about how grandparents have blessed his daughter Maggie. "Maggie is fortunate enough to have four grandparents who are all supportive in numerous ways. Sometimes they do simple things like picking her up from school or taking her to one of her therapies when we have a conflict of schedules. Other times their help is more specific to her condition."

Maggie struggles with math because of the intellectual disabilities common to Down syndrome. "When my dad learned that there was a math book for students with Down, he bought it, read it, and immediately started tutoring Maggie in math," Mark said. "We thought once or twice a week would be more than enough, but Maggie loves it so much that she's always asking if Gramps can come over and 'do math' with her. I think it also has to do with the point reward system he set up so they can go out for ice cream."

Be available, and you'll find that building trust over time by continuously offering your help will make all the difference in the world. Mark's dad had a talent that he could use in a specific way to benefit his granddaughter. Instead of fights and frustration over math homework, Gramps was able to instill in Maggie a love for math—and for him. That's an investment that will last a lifetime.

Investing at Church

One Sunday morning, a pastor welcomed a young mother to the worship service with her preschool-age son. During the service, her son began crying, which quickly escalated into a full meltdown. Struggling to get hold of her son, the mother tried to navigate him through the row of chairs and out of the sanctuary. It was obvious to everyone that the boy was making things very difficult for her.

The pastor, who had not yet entered the service, turned toward the commotion in the foyer to see the frantic mother with her distraught son wrapped in her arms. He warmly invited her and her son to sit with him. When the boy calmed down a little, the young lady poured out her story as her son began playing on the floor.

She told about her struggles with her son's diagnosis of autism and how his father had become disconnected and eventually absent. This was a woman who desperately needed to experience the love of Christ and the communion of the saints in that moment. What would have happened had the pastor not been there and responded in the way he did? It's entirely possible that she would have walked out of church altogether, unseen by anyone, and might never have returned.

There are too many stories about how churches have put up barriers for families of children with disabilities. In some churches, these families are made to feel unwanted. In most cases, however, it isn't that a local congregation doesn't care. They simply have no idea that they are neglecting the most vulnerable in their midst. They have forgotten that Jesus' parable of the great banquet in Luke 14 is for us today.

In this story, Jesus makes it clear that everyone is invited to the "great feast" of salvation—including "the poor, the crippled, the blind, and the lame" (verse 21). The body of Christ is not about "whole" people showing each other how well they are doing. It is a community of broken people sharing with each other the joy of salvation and their Source of strength in Jesus Christ. When we exclude people from our churches, we are the ones who lose. Diversity is God's design. Our churches need to understand this, regardless of the size of the church and whether it has an official program for those with special needs.

As you can see from this pastor's encounter, "huge" investments aren't necessarily large in terms of quantity (or financial cost). Recall the one talent given to the servant in Jesus' parable in Matthew 25:14-30. All that was required for it to be significant in the master's eyes was that it be invested. Something as simple as being available for childcare in your church can make an immense difference for couples and marriages.

Forget the Myths

Some stories shared in this chapter might seem extraordinarily heroic. Most of the time, however, grandparents don't have to be "superhuman" to help their families or their churches. And don't fall for some common myths that tend to derail our efforts.

Myth 1: Long-distance relationships don't work.

Families can continue to flourish regardless of the physical distance between them. Many grandchildren living far away from their grandparents are thriving because they're able to stay well connected. They have found ways to be a vital part of their grandchildren's lives. Technology makes it possible to remain close and involved like never before.

Myth 2: Working grandparents miss out.

Grandparents who work full time can still find meaningful, valuable ways to connect and make a difference. While the amount of time spent with grandchildren is important, it is more important to love *well* with the time you do have to invest in them.

Myth 3: Our family is too disorganized.

Flexibility and expecting the unexpected can go a long way. While none of us really has total control over our own life, families with disability in the mix rarely enjoy the luxury of being in control of their schedules. They have no delusions about that. When you realize you probably won't have things just the way you might like but are willing to step into the gap anyway, the reward will be enjoying a bigger part in the lives of all your grandchildren.

Myth 4: My grandchild doesn't appreciate me.

A Christlike attitude is everything. When you fully accept your grandchild as a person made in the image of God and when you see her as a blessing, you open the door for productive interaction with all of your family. Even if you aren't thanked, you can forgive ungratefulness and be involved at some level.

And ask yourself, *What is the alternative?* No involvement means no investment—and no rewards—for anyone.

John Bunyan is quoted as saying in one of his sermons, "Seamen cannot create the wind, but they can hoist their sails to welcome it." The rewards can be huge if the sails are set to catch the wind. What sails are you hoisting in the wind for the sake of your grandchild?

A Heritage of Faith

Ultimately, investment is about heritage, and there is no more important part of one's heritage than a legacy of faith in Christ and the gospel. As a grandparent, you are uniquely positioned to help your grandchild develop a vibrant and growing faith in the Lord. Indeed, this heritage is perhaps the greatest gift you can pass on to your descendants. As you serve your children and grandchildren faithfully, rest assured that the Lord is using you to plant seeds that can bear fruit for a lifetime to come.

Supporting a Special-Needs Ministry

Grandparents can play a vital part in helping churches demonstrate God's heart toward vulnerable families. We can be advocates for our grandchildren and for all children. Jesus said, "Let the children come to me. Don't stop them!" (Matthew 19:14)—and this includes children with special needs. If your church is not already addressing this, here are some ways you can become involved:

- Talk to your pastor and church leaders about hosting a Disability Awareness Sunday. Discuss ways to help God's people understand His heart for all people, including special-needs children, and how they can help.

- Seek out those in your church who are already a part of the disability community. If your church is small, you might encounter some who say, "Our church doesn't have anyone with a disability." But often, these families *are* in your church; it's simply that no one has noticed. Seek them out and spend time hearing their stories. Build a community of support and friendship around them.

- Invite others to be part of your grassroots efforts to build up those who face special challenges in your faith community. Determine how you will welcome and include new families and individuals who visit your church. One of the best places to learn about how to support special-needs families is to contact Joni and Friends at www.joniandfriends.org/church-relations. This worldwide ministry equips churches with great ideas and resources to get started. Educate your congregation on the blessings they are missing by not getting to know these families.

Your investment in your church can reap huge rewards. One mother said it well: "My daughter attends a special-needs ministry in our church where she is welcomed with loving arms every week. The most amazing people have entered our lives . . . and each has brought an amazing gift, a lesson, a blessing to us."

Imagine this in your church. This kind of legacy will be powerful not just for your own family but for the whole community as well.

16

Building a Godly Heritage

We will not hide these truths from our children; we will tell the next generation about the glorious deeds of the LORD, about his power and his mighty wonders.

PSALM 78:4

Only the living can praise you as I do today. Each generation tells of your faithfulness to the next.

ISAIAH 38:19

Good people leave an inheritance to their grandchildren.

PROVERBS 13:22

❦

A SURVEY OF AMERICAN MILLIONAIRES conducted by CNBC reported that more than half of them plan to leave each of their children $1 million or more. Of those with $5 million or more, one in five said they would leave their kids at least $100 million.

The numbers reflect "a massive cascade of wealth" that could pour down on high-profile kids for generations to come.[1] It begs the question, "Along with passing down material wealth, what values will these parents pass on to their children?"

Heritage is most often thought of as material gain,

especially in the reading of a person's last will and testament. But heritage is far more than property or valuable objects. It could even be argued that whatever *heritage* is passed on, it always includes the psychological and spiritual DNA of past generations. Heritage matters—for good or evil. While wealth and riches may come and go, it's how one lives—our character, reputation, and faith—that will truly outlive us.

Proverbs 13:22 says, "Good people leave an inheritance to their grandchildren, but the sinner's wealth passes to the godly." At first glance, it appears this proverb is only speaking about material wealth. But is it? Notice that good people leave an "inheritance" for generations to come, but the sinner leaves only wealth, which eventually defaults to the righteous. By implication, a *good* person leaves a *good* inheritance that will bless even his or her grandchildren, while wicked people leave nothing but material wealth, which not even their descendants will enjoy.

So what constitutes the inheritance of a good person? Scripture speaks much more about the importance of attaining wisdom, virtue, character, and faith over money, and it portrays a strong contrast between *inheritance* and *wealth*. In truth, we will all leave a legacy of some kind, but a godly heritage doesn't happen by chance; we must be intentional if we want to pass on our faith to the next generation.

> Every boy and girl has the capacity to grasp the heart of spiritual things.

As grandparents, it's possible to support our families emotionally, financially, and relationally—all important and meaningful—and still miss the most important area: spiritual support. The legacy of faith we pass on to our children and grandchildren is the one thing that matters in both this life and the life to come.

Your grandchild with special needs may not be able to comprehend everything about a life of faith, but every boy and girl has the capacity to grasp the heart of spiritual things. Just like you, your granddaughter is fully able to have a relationship with her Creator. The Father says His will is that none of the *little ones* should perish (Matthew 18:14). If she is that important to Him, why would you not do all you can to be a conduit of God's grace in her life?

One Grandfather's Legacy

John believes that his father, Harlan, is the godliest man he has ever known. Even when John doubted God's goodness, feeling like life was one long string of unending disappointments, his father would say, "It's going to be okay, son. My God will supply all your needs. If you don't believe that, let me hold on to that for you." It was not a sappy response, but one that communicated to John that his father understood he faced hard things in the world, and that he could trust his father would never abandon him.

John's son Paul was born with multiple disabilities, including, among others, anophthalmia (lack of eyes), growth hormone deficiencies, and intellectual disabilities. John admits he did not deal well with the reality. He maintained a facade for about three months, but after one particularly hard surgery, he'd had enough.

"I never stopped believing in God; I just didn't believe He was good," John explains. "I said mean things about God to others out of my own self-righteousness."

John pulled his family out of a good church, admitting

(in retrospect) that he was not a kind man back then. Feeling anchorless for a season, he still took care of his son and was there for all the medical procedures. Yet John constantly felt like his life was a train wreck and that he'd probably built his faith on false pretenses. His belief system was based upon the lie that if he did good things, God somehow owed him. His son's struggles didn't fit with the deal John thought he'd made with God.

Throughout this experience, John's parents were his rock. His father was, in John's words, "the first one who got my son correctly. He saw him as a boy in our family—not cursed, but simply a boy God made like all the other boys." When Grandpa Harlan held his grandson for the first time, he gently declared, "If the only reason I was put on this earth was to be your grandfather, that's good enough for me."

John's parents continued to show their love in other ways, including driving fifteen hours to the hospital where their grandson Paul was having surgery. They not only made the long drive but also brought along a rocking chair so the whole family could take turns rocking little Paul. They were persistent and encouraging while John was struggling.

"Dad kept telling me how much he loved me, how much he loved my wife and his grandson, and he encouraged me to love my wife and son. He always said he was praying for me," John shared.

Despite John's anger and bitterness, his parents continued to love and support him, until one day he recognized his desperation and need for a Savior. John says, "I knew that the Bible was full of lament, sorrow, and doubt. But suddenly I understood that when we bring our suffering before the throne of God, He understands. God does provide for all your needs.[2] He owns the cattle on a thousand hills.[3]

Should I not believe He can provide for me today and in the future?"

John rejoices that he now has the privilege of coming alongside others who are in similar places of need, to do for them what his parents and others did for him. His story is a beautiful reminder of the importance of a spiritual heritage rooted in the truth of the Scriptures.

The Fellowship of Suffering

As grandparents, our adult children may not always treat us well amid their suffering and hurt, but we can still be there for them. We can show them that no matter what happens, we love them, and God loves them. We demonstrate that "in all these things we are more than conquerors through him who loved us," that "neither death nor life, neither angels nor demons, neither the present nor the future, nor any powers, neither height nor depth, nor anything else in all creation, will be able to separate us from the love of God that is in Christ Jesus our Lord" (Romans 8:37-39, NIV).

It is easy to forget that a spiritual heritage requires a partnership of one generation with another. The greatest impact we can have on our grandchildren, with or without disabilities, is when parents and grandparents are united in exhibiting the life of Christ and the gospel. To make this happen, we must be intentional.

In his final sermon, Moses warned the Israelites, "Watch out! Be careful never to forget what you yourself have seen. Do not let these memories escape from your mind as long as you live! And be sure to pass them on to your children and grand-children" (Deuteronomy 4:9). God told Joshua as they were about to face the giants in the land once more, "Be strong and courageous! Do not be afraid or discouraged. For the LORD your God is with you wherever you go" (Joshua 1:9).

Do you believe these things? Do your children and grand-children know you believe them? John's father believed them enough that he could say, in effect, "Even if you don't believe them, I will hold on to them for both of us."

You can strive to create a consistent environment of faith, hope, and love in your family, beginning with words of appreciation for your adult children and their spouses. Of course, this is the ideal. Sometimes you may feel alone in your efforts to spiritually influence your family. How do you build a spiritual heritage for your grandchild in that situation? How do you cultivate a legacy of faith for a grandchild who has very limited capacities?

How to Leave a Legacy of Faith

When Linda's daughter-in-law heard the cerebral palsy diagnosis for her daughter, Kammy Jo, she said, "I can't do this." Linda and her husband, Jack, however, supported her.

"I told her, 'Yes, you can. We're going to get through this together.' In that moment, we received a peace and assurance that God would give us what we needed," Linda says. "We cried and held Kammy Jo. The entire family prayed and agreed we would all do whatever needed to be done."

Linda and Jack understood that building a spiritual heritage for Kammy Jo would be one of their most important roles and challenges. For a time, when the three lived in their home, it was easy for Linda to integrate Bible stories and conversation into their daily lives. Once the kids moved into their own home, it required more intentionality. Now when they're together, Linda sings songs to her granddaughter because she loves music. Kammy Jo also loves to pray, and they make it a point to pray over her, with her, and for her as much as possible. During overnight stays, they enjoy more time together. Kammy Jo looks forward to reading with her grandparents and listening to them share Bible stories.

While every family has their unique characteristics, there are several common essentials that any grandparent can use to pass on a godly heritage to his or her grandchild. These apply to children with or without disabilities.

Embrace a Godly Perspective

The attitude of the heart is the beginning point. Cultivating a godly heritage starts with a godly perspective of the child God has placed in your care. If you believe God is not good, but cruel, then you will see your grandchild as a cruel mistake. But God does not make mistakes. In fact, ponder these questions God asked Moses: "Who makes a person's mouth? Who decides whether people speak or do not speak, hear or do not hear, see or do not see? Is it not I, the LORD?" (Exodus 4:11).

God is not embarrassed or ashamed by your grandchild's disability. All children are precious gifts and should be celebrated. See your grandchild as a child of God who needs to be loved and who can teach you how to love more deeply. This is the way to indescribable joy and a heritage that matters.

Breathe the Glory

As we've observed previously, grandparents experience a measure of double-suffering that provides an opportunity to display double-glory. We suffer for our adult children, who sometimes carry a 24/7 burden for a child with special needs. We also feel the distress of our grandchildren, who may never experience the carefree life of their peers. But there is glory in knowing God's power can be displayed in both your adult children and grandchildren in ways that you may not have imagined. It can also be an opportunity to show society that (as one father masterfully put it) you do not "breathe the cultural air" of pity or disdain for those who bring disabled children into the world. Be a person who breathes the fresh air of God's glory and rejoices over your grandchild.

Celebrate with Prayer and Worship

Pray often for, with, and over your grandchild and adult children. Tell them, "I am praying for you every day. I love you." At the Christian Grandparenting Network,[4] you can find "Scriptures to Pray for Your Grandchildren" cards as well as weekly prayer suggestions for grandparents. These are great tools to help focus on Scriptures you can use for daily prayer.

Singing worship songs together is another good way to build a godly legacy with your grandchildren. Sing songs with them that exalt God and declare the truth of His love, grace, and sovereignty. Maybe you don't fancy yourself a singer. Do it anyway. If your singing makes the cat hide under the bed, then buy a few kids' worship CDs your grandchild would enjoy.

Plant Seeds of Truth

God promises that His Word will not return to Him empty or void (Isaiah 55:11). When you read Scriptures and Bible stories to your grandchildren, you impress God's truth upon their hearts and minds, even if you don't think they understand. Let God decide how He will use His Word. Your job is to speak it, and if they are able, help them memorize it.

The fact that your adult children may be doing a good job of teaching and discipling your grandchild doesn't excuse you from also being involved. God makes it clear you are to teach your children *and* your grandchildren. Discuss with your adult children how you can reinforce and complement what they are already doing.

Demonstrate Self-Sacrifice

What are you willing to give up so you can do something for your grandchild? Jesus said He came "not to be served but to serve others" (Matthew 20:28). Imagine the heritage that is passed on by those whose lives are committed to serving.

Ron and Cookie sold their home and moved to another state, away from their friends and all that was familiar, in order to be close to their granddaughter and son. Their granddaughter, Samantha, may not understand all that they did until she is older, but their sacrifice is a legacy that will outlive them.

In contrast, imagine the legacy that will follow grandparents who, when confronted with a dramatic medical change in their grandchild, responded to pleas for help by saying that they had enough on their plates and had already done their years of child rearing.

A godly heritage is one that humbly puts the interests of others above its own, especially when it comes to family.

Be a Conduit of Blessing

Speak words of blessing over your children and grandchildren often. Intercessory prayer is speaking to God on behalf of another. A spoken blessing is speaking to another on behalf of God. The Father spoke from heaven over Jesus saying, "You are my Son, whom I love; with you I am well pleased" (Mark 1:11, NIV). Who wouldn't want to hear a parent or grandparent speak words of affirmation over him or her?

Since the time that Cavin Harper's grandson, Corban, was very young, Cavin has intentionally spoken words of blessing over him. It was usually a simple recitation of the Aaronic blessing in Numbers 6:24-26: "The LORD bless you and keep you; the LORD make his face shine on you and be gracious to you; the LORD turn his face toward you and give you peace" (NIV). And then Grandpa Cavin would add, "We are so pleased to be your grandparents!"

Because of his Asperger's, Corban would often hide under the covers. Sometimes he would fidget and squirm because touchy-feely things were very awkward for him. But his grandparents kept saying the blessings because they knew it was important that Corban know how much he is valued by his grandparents and God, and that God had already marked out a purpose for him.

Their grandson Corban is now a teenager. Recently he wrote this short piece for a school project. It was a powerful and tear-filled confirmation that he really does understand his true identity.

Dear God, I don't want to get confused as to what my identity is. I don't want to think that I am anything less than a child of God, Creator of all things. I am a child of You, Lord, that is who I am. Likewise, I don't want to base my identity, my worth, on what other people think, but on what You think of me instead. And don't let me forget how dependent I am on You either. This is who I, Corban, truly am . . . A Child of God. "

How do you view your grandson or granddaughter with special needs? Do you see this child as God's gift—a boy or girl just like all the other boys and girls made with hearts, souls, and minds by the Father's touch? Like all children, your grandchild needs to be loved and to know that the Creator treasures her. It's why Jesus died for her sins just as He did ours, why He rose from the grave so He could give her life and hope, and why He's coming again to make everything new. Now that's a godly heritage!

Planting Seeds of Faith

A farmer went out to plant some seeds.

MATTHEW 13:3

Ask God to prepare the soil of your grandchild's heart to know God and to bear good fruit. Watch and listen for his response to discussions about God and His Word. Depending on a child's age, here are some barriers he might need to overcome:

Seeds on the road: "I hear the Word of God, but I don't understand it."

Seeds in the rocks: "I want to follow Jesus, but it seems too hard for me."

Seeds among the thorns: "Maybe God does care, but I struggle with too much other stuff."

What Children Need to Know

- "God loves me just the way I am because He made me in His image." *Genesis 1:27*
- "I am a sinner and will ask Jesus to forgive me. Sin is breaking God's laws." *1 John 3:4*

- "Jesus gave His life for me so I could be in God's forever family." *John 3:16*

Ways to Share the Gospel with Your Grandchild

1. Young children can tell Jesus they are sorry by singing simple songs. This one is to the tune of "Frère Jacques":

I am sorry, I am sorry.
I was wrong, I was wrong.
Will you please forgive me?
Will you please forgive me?
Let's be friends, let's be friends!

2. Read these wonderful picture books to young children, who will enjoy hearing them again and again.

The Crippled Lamb, by Max Lucado (Thomas Nelson)
You Are Special, by Max Lucado (Crossway)
Thank You, God, for Loving Me, by Max Lucado (Tommy Nelson)
Wait until Then, by Randy Alcorn (Tyndale)
The Parable of the Lily, by Liz Curtis Higgs (Tommy Nelson)
God Gave Us Easter, by Lisa Tawn Bergren (WaterBrook)

Older children will enjoy The Chronicles of Narnia, by C. S. Lewis (HarperCollins).

3. Act out and discuss Bible drama skits with your
   grandchildren.

The Wise Man and the Foolish Man—
   Matthew 7:24-27, Luke 6:47-49
The Pearl of Great Price—Matthew 13:45-46
The Lost Sheep—Matthew 18:12-14, Luke 15:3-7
Jesus Talks with a Samaritan Woman—John 4:1-26
The Resurrection—Luke 24:1-12

4. Teach the "Roman Road to Salvation." Older
   children can look up Bible verses, make road signs,
   and share them with their family. Ask children to put
   the verses in their own words.

STOP: Romans 3:23
U-TURN: Romans 6:23
YIELD: Romans 5:6
ONE WAY: Romans 10:9
GO: Romans 8:16

5. Evangelism tools for kids

The EvangeCube: www.christianbook.com
   /page/church/outreach/evangecube
The Gospel Bracelet: www.pinterest.com
   /explore/salvation-bracelet
Resurrection Eggs: www.familylife.com
   /resurrectioneggs

Knowing God satisfies a child's needs for

- unconditional love,
- belonging (he or she becomes part of God's family),
- order and purpose in the world, and
- hope in times of darkness.

Invite your grandchildren into your life of faith and introduce them to your Savior!

More fun family activities on teaching prayer and Bible memory to children can be found on our website at www .joniandfriends.org/real-families-real-needs.

PART 5

A Family Member's Support

17

Acceptance and Inclusion

When our infant daughter Abby was diagnosed with diabetes, several family members took the initiative to learn about her condition. They invested time in researching her needs and even learned how to administer Abby's insulin shots. Because they were trained, we felt confident that Abby would be okay staying with them when my husband and I had the opportunity to travel to London for ten days.

We were also blessed to have friends who were willing to watch our daughter for brief periods of time when we were a phone call away, but it was family who put the extra effort into learning how to care for Abby so we could still have time away as a couple. Their willingness to embrace our child and her diabetes made us feel loved and more connected to our family than ever before.

KIM—MOTHER OF ABBY

❦

MARY JANE HAD A ZEAL for life from the moment she took her first breath. The doctors told her parents that cerebral palsy would likely claim her life before she learned to walk or talk, but Mary Jane proved them wrong. As she grew, her family refused to let her be defined by her diagnosis and simply treated Mary Jane the same as her sister. No one called her *crippled*, which was a common term when Mary Jane was young.

That was, until her fourth grade teacher labeled her as such and had Mary Jane removed from the neighborhood elementary school. While her teacher's words and actions hurt deeply, Mary Jane's early years had given her confidence to push back against unfair labels and low expectations.

In the early to mid-1900s, when Mary Jane was a child, most children and adults with disabilities were institutionalized away from the nurturing influences of their families. Mary Jane, in contrast, benefited from a secure home environment. Buoyed by the sense of potential her family instilled in her, Mary Jane believed she could make a difference as a missionary in China. Decades later, she did just that, taking the gospel to people with disabilities in China and around the world.

While peers and teachers shape a person's self-image in dramatic ways, family members are the most powerful influencers. Aunts and uncles, grandparents, and cousins all form what is for many children the first environment for social inclusion and acceptance. Thanksgiving dinners, family weddings or funerals, informal get-togethers, or full-blown family reunions serve as a child's first foundry for hammering out what is expected in social gatherings.

The people in your social circles are largely there by choice. When it comes to family, things are different. With few exceptions, we have no say in who makes up the branches of our family trees. But we still have to decide whether we will intentionally welcome and include a grandchild, niece, nephew, or cousin with a disability. If you are unprepared to do this, you may find that you have also rejected those you love most.

Inclusion 101

How can you be more welcoming? How can you create a safe haven for your family member with a disability? For starters, focus on the person rather than the diagnosis.

Leah's daughter Becky was born with a cleft palate. She was grateful for the support from her family before and after the surgery to correct Becky's palate. It healed quickly, but every time their family gathered, Leah's aunt would look at Becky's scar and comment on it. While Leah believed her aunt meant well, her constant attention to the scar made it seem that all she saw was the former cleft palate—not Becky. Leah wondered if her aunt even noticed Becky's wonderful traits, such as her sense of humor and her engaging smile.

It can be natural to want to ask questions and learn more about a family member's health issues, but proceed with caution. For some children, the family setting may be the only place where they don't feel different or experience stares or comments. For others, family may not be a safe place either.

"In the last couple years of my son Shane's life, my sister-in-law visited with her little girl and encouraged her to climb up in his wheelchair to talk with him. Not only did encouraging that relationship between the cousins mean a lot to Shane as well as to my husband and me, but I also know that my niece will grow up being more comfortable around people with disabilities."

Carissa Mortensen, disability ministries pastor, Grace Fellowship Church

In a blog for Key Ministry, one mother confessed that she sometimes dreads larger family gatherings because relatives who barely know her child feel the need to voice uninformed opinions: "'You need to stop babying him.'" "'You knew this was a risk when you had kids, but you just had to have kids anyway.'" "'Have you tried putting her on meds?'"

Yet she goes on to challenge us to keep participating, to keep showing up at family functions, because the adage about not being able to "change the culture" if we don't "engage in the culture" also applies to families.[1]

Gracie found that it helped to keep family members informed about her son's limitations. Jeremiah has a condition called Arthrogryposis Multiplex Congenita, and he was born with a dislocated hip, bilateral clubbed feet, scoliosis, and flexed wrists. He's had several surgeries and countless hours of therapy.

"The most helpful thing we have done for our family is to explain in detail (often with pictures) Jeremiah's limitations and abilities," Gracie said. "I've done this several times so his relatives know how to treat him. As a boy, he loves to wrestle and sword fight, but he cannot move or take a blow like most kids. Keeping his balance is still challenging, and yet he finds ways to fall safely and have fun with the rest of us."

A child's parents and siblings will usually be the most knowledgeable about his or her abilities and limitations. Extended family members may have firsthand information that can make inclusion easier, or they may need to welcome the child affected by a disability without extensive knowledge of his diagnosis. The rule is to trust the experts—the parents who are with the child every day! Even when you believe you have an adequate understanding about the situation, err on the side of believing those who are present with the child most. For children with disabilities, health changes may occur on a regular basis.

Gracie worked hard to help educate her family so they could support Jeremiah in the best possible way. "Jeremiah must learn to limit himself and figure out how to manage life skills on his own," Gracie said. "We shared this way of parenting and life philosophy with our family and model it for them. We urge them to support us rather than criticize and judge. They try to be helpful, but ultimately the most loving thing for them to do is to listen well to the information we offer them about Jeremiah and do their best to support and uphold what we believe is best for our family."

The ABCs of Accommodation

Accommodation is a key aspect of inclusion. If we want to be inclusive and welcoming to our family members with disabilities, then we must find ways to accommodate their special needs without drawing unnecessary attention to them. This may require environmental changes, such as placing a temporary ramp of two-by-four planks over your front steps or removing the rug and magazine rack in the bathroom for a person using a walker or wheelchair.

Accommodation can also include changes in our attitudes. We must be willing to accept and acknowledge how our loved one's disability will affect travel, play, and mealtimes. Some people, like Gracie's son Jeremiah, have learned how to do many things for themselves. Others require more help from those around them. Where do we start in our efforts toward accommodation and inclusion? Remember the ABCs: Ask; Be available; Carry on.

Ask

The best way to know how you can be helpful is to hear it straight from your loved one. You might try asking questions such as

- Is there anything that would be helpful for me to know?
- Would it be easier for you if we got together at the park or a restaurant?
- Is there anything we could do to make your time more successful and enjoyable?

Rachel regrets that she didn't think to ask her sister Julie these questions before a family picnic to celebrate birthdays. Julie's son Lukas can't handle wide-open spaces. Instead of enjoying their family time together, Julie spent most of the day chasing Lukas to keep him from heading out into the street.

Be Available

Once you have asked how you can help, make sure you are available to follow through! Be sure your communication style reveals a willing attitude that will encourage your loved one to mention any additional needs that may arise during an activity.

Carry On

It isn't necessary to make someone's disability the center of attention, even when you're focused on meeting his or her need. For example, when lifting a wheelchair up the front steps into the house, consider that your loved one may be embarrassed by all of the extra attention and effort exerted on his behalf. Try to keep a casual, "no big deal" attitude as much as possible.

As the host of an inclusive family party, you'll need to be flexible and ready to make changes or adjustments. Assess the party environment and know that your family members with disabilities might need to come late and/or leave early. Assure them that you understand and it is not a problem. If there is a wheelchair user coming, make sure there is ample room for him at the table and to maneuver around and participate as much as possible.

Food allergies, as well as any environmental sensitivities such as noises or scents, can ruin the fun. If you cannot accommodate your family member's specific dietary needs, let her know that she is welcome to bring her own food. Be sure to designate room in the refrigerator or oven for her dishes. If you've determined that your family member can become overstimulated, it's a great idea to prepare an empty room or a quiet, safe space where your loved one can rest or calm down.[2]

A Faulty Belief System

For many, the biggest hindrance to making sure a loved one feels truly valued and accepted is a faulty belief system. The value of all human life—including those with a disability—has come under fire in our culture. Doubts and questions regarding the "quality of life" of persons with disabilities are now commonplace.

As a result, some well-meaning Christians have begun to wonder if an individual with a disability would be "better off dead" or "better off never having been born in the first place," leading them to seriously contemplate the moral acceptability of abortion and euthanasia to "prevent" the disability and the suffering that is sometimes associated with it.

These thoughts and practices are, however, contrary to a

biblical worldview. Scripture assures us in Genesis 1:27 that *every* human being is created in the image of God and is therefore of immense worth.

Do you have the faith to believe that God allows disabilities so His power can be seen in the world? In John 9:3, Jesus explained that a certain man's blindness was not a punishment for sin, but that it "happened so the power of God could be seen in him."

Jesus frequently stopped to speak to and touch people with disabilities. King David modeled this when he sought out Mephibosheth, the disabled son of Jonathan, and gave him a place of honor at his table (see 2 Samuel 9).

Have you secretly suspected that your family member with a disability is more of a burden than a blessing? Have you questioned whether it might be better if your loved one simply passed quietly in his or her sleep? If so, please pray for God to change your perspective and help you provide the love he or she deserves.

Joni Eareckson Tada knows firsthand that life can still have tremendous value and those with disabilities can bring God much glory if given the opportunity. "We have a special obligation to protect the weak and protect the vulnerable in our society," Joni said, "because God created us, and we are of equal dignity, and we are not at each other's disposal. The weak and the vulnerable need their rights safeguarded."[3]

If this is an area you wrestle with, take the time to challenge your deep-seated beliefs with truths from God's Word. This topic is addressed in the *Beyond Suffering: A Christian View on Disability Ministry* study guide created by Joni and Friends, which also provides a recommended-resources section with books and videos that help explain the value of all human life according to Scripture.[4] For additional

information and resources, visit www.joniandfriends
.org/real-families-real-needs.

Better Than Inclusion

Ultimately, what we want for our loved ones with disabilities
is better than inclusion—we want their success. The online
Merriam-Webster Dictionary defines *handicap*, when used
as a verb, as follows: "to make success or progress difficult
for (someone)."[5] Many individuals with disabilities say it's
society's attitudes that impede their success more than their
actual impairments.

Ellen Stumbo has three daughters, two of whom have
disabilities. In a blog post titled "Why Are We So Afraid of
Disability?" she examined how society, even family, sometimes responds negatively to those with special needs. Fear,
ignorance, and a lack of personal experience with disability
are at the root of these negative responses.

A small first step Ellen has taken is to encourage questions and natural curiosity, rather than scolding or taking
offense when someone stares at her daughters. Ellen wants
to help the next generation learn the valuable lesson her
daughters have taught her—"to recognize that the value of
life is not found in who we are not, it is found in who we
already are."[6]

Just as Mary Jane's family refused to let cerebral palsy
define who she is or keep her from ministering in China, we,
too, can embrace and support our loved ones so that they
know their real value. We can encourage those with disabilities toward success. We can trust that Ephesians 2:10 is not
just for some of us, but for *all*: "We are God's masterpiece.
He has created us anew in Christ Jesus, so we can do the good
things he planned for us long ago."

How to Make Loved Ones with Disabilities Feel at Ease

- Ask before helping; don't make assumptions.
- It's okay to ask people about their disabilities, but understand that they may not want to talk about them. Make small talk about things they enjoy as you would with anyone.
- Just because a person uses a wheelchair doesn't mean she is sick or helpless. Many people who use wheelchairs are healthy and strong.
- When you're talking with a person in a wheelchair, sit down so his neck won't become sore looking up at you.
- It's okay to ask your loved one with a speech problem to repeat what she said if you didn't understand the first time.
- If your loved one is using an interpreter to speak with you, make sure you talk to your loved one, not the interpreter.
- Don't speak loudly when talking to a blind person. He can hear as well as you.
- Never pet or play with service animals unless you've gained permission. They can't be distracted from the job they are doing.
- Think about ways to make sure each family member can be included in the activities you do.[7]

18

Standing in the Gap

My husband, David, and I were not yet dating when he called me at work. I was a little embarrassed that he was willing to use my work line for a personal call until I realized he wasn't calling to flirt. His mother had a leak in her spinal column and had become partially paralyzed. Since I worked at Joni and Friends, he wondered if I had any resources I could direct his family to.

I never imagined my first interaction with my future mother-in-law would be in a professional rather than personal capacity. But of course, that wasn't the end of it. Several months later, David and I were visiting his mother at a local park when making it to a restroom became an urgent matter.

In the unfamiliar circumstances of the public bathroom, she needed assistance. David would have done anything that needed doing, but he was as new to her needs as I was. I wanted to preserve their typical mother-son relationship as much as I could.

I felt so out of my element. I barely knew David's mom and didn't have any special training in personal caregiving. But I served the needs of the moment and helped a mother and son as they worked through the new dynamics brought about by her disability. It meant a lot to both of them that I was willing to be a part of meeting even the most intimate needs of the family.

REBECCA OLSON—DAUGHTER-IN-LAW

IN TODAY'S AMERICAN CULTURE, the extended family plays a smaller role in a person's life than perhaps at any other time in history. More often than not, the reality of our increasingly mobile society has meant families are scattered and disconnected.

When an out-of-state family member needs help, it can be tempting to let ourselves off the hook or make excuses. We can even point to a biblical justification: "Do not forsake your friend or a friend of your family, and do not go to your relative's house when disaster strikes you—better a neighbor nearby than a relative far away" (Proverbs 27:10, NIV). We may tell ourselves, *Surely there must be someone closer who can help.*

> Throughout Scripture we see examples of love and sacrifice and going the extra mile for family.

The point of this verse is to highlight the importance of building and maintaining supportive friendships, not to devalue the role of family. We can certainly agree that in the midst of a crisis, it is easier to have help close at hand rather than to wait for help to come from a distance. But make no mistake—the Bible is not quiet on the topic of offering assistance to relatives. Throughout Scripture, we see examples of love and sacrifice and going the extra mile for family.

Abraham and Lot

Perhaps you're familiar with the story of Abraham and his nephew Lot traveling far from their homeland and settling in neighboring regions. The Bible doesn't indicate whether there was any interaction between them once they parted ways in a time before cell phones and when travel was arduous.

In Genesis 18, the Lord tells Abraham that He plans to destroy Sodom and Gomorrah—with Sodom being the very place where Lot had settled. The cities had such a reputation for wickedness that the Lord could not allow it any longer.

In a scene unlike any other, Abraham bargains with the Lord, pleading with Him to preserve the cities if He could find ten righteous people living there. God ultimately destroys both cities, but Abraham's petitions on behalf of his nephew do not go unanswered.

Genesis 19:29 says, "God had listened to Abraham's request and kept Lot safe, removing him from the disaster that engulfed the cities on the plain." Abraham's prayers from a distance were powerful and effective.

Ruth and Naomi

The book of Ruth opens with Naomi relocating to the land of Moab with her husband and two sons. Tragedy strikes and all three men die in the foreign land. Naomi is left destitute and decides to return to Israel.

At first, both of her daughters-in-law decide to come with her, but at Naomi's urging, Orpah turns back. Ruth, however, remains devoted. Over the course of Naomi's story, Ruth proves herself to be so loyal that she earns the attention of Boaz,[1] a distant relative.

He compliments Ruth, saying, "I also know about everything you have done for your mother-in-law since the death of your husband" (Ruth 2:11). Boaz accepts the role of kinsman-redeemer and marries Ruth.

Both Boaz and Ruth went above and beyond what their culture expected of their family responsibilities. Together, they provided Naomi with a grandchild, Obed, who became grandfather to King David, in the line of the Messiah.

Even observers who did not have the advantage of history to see the glorious results of their loyalty praised God for such dedication to family. Naomi's neighbors all agreed that her daughter-in-law had been better to her than seven sons.[2]

Esther and Mordecai

Another inspiring tale of family caregiving is told in the book of Esther. Esther was orphaned at a young age. Her older cousin Mordecai adopted her and raised her. He could have considered his task complete as soon as she was taken from his home and given to the king for his harem, but Mordecai didn't step back from supporting Esther.

Instead, he daily walked near the courtyard of the harem to hear news of her. After she became queen, he continued to offer support and guidance.[3] Esther relied heavily on Mordecai's advice, which led to her saving not only the life of the king but also the lives of all the Jews in Persia.

True Religion

In each of these stories, an individual showed dedication far beyond the cultural expectations of normal family ties. When these relatives stepped in to help, God's people were rescued and God was glorified. The same is true today!

Although the family caring for a child with disabilities is probably not facing God's wrath or possible annihilation, they could probably use support and encouragement. They may be wrestling with feelings of isolation or rejection. They may be exhausted from carrying the weight of constant caregiving, therapies, or meltdowns. Most likely, they need a family member to come alongside them to hold up their hands, as Aaron and Hur did for Moses, allowing the Israelites to defeat their enemy (Exodus 17:11-13).

Families like these yearn for their relatives to provide a support system that is there for them no matter what. In her book *Get Your Joy Back*, author Laurie Wallin writes about the sense of abandonment shared by many parents of special-needs children when there is no one to stand in the gap for them:

> No matter how old we are, no matter how well our families of origin have gotten along, deep down we long for our families to support us unconditionally . . . and forever. To include us, even if we ourselves or our kids are high maintenance. To treat us as though they're on our team, even if they don't understand why we parent the way we do or why our kids don't progress according to traditional models of development. We expect them to be as up to the task of loving us and our kids as our circumstances require us to be. When they can't or won't fill that expectation, at the very least we can feel emotionally abandoned.[4]

Many Christians have a passion to address social justice issues—which is awesome—but we also can't lose sight of the call to minister to the needs within our own families. Isaiah 58:7 says, "Share your food with the hungry, and give shelter to the homeless. Give clothes to those who need them, and *do not hide from relatives who need your help*" (emphasis added).

In 1 Timothy 5:8, Paul's charge to Timothy makes it clear that caring for relatives is an expected part of living out our faith. Paul writes, "Those who won't care for their relatives, especially those in their own household, have denied the true faith. Such people are worse than unbelievers."

Those are harsh words, especially as the many needs associated with a disability can seem overwhelming. Where do we begin? It can be as simple as making a phone call to tell your sister you're available if she needs to talk, or sending your nephew an e-mail inviting his family to dinner and asking about his son's dietary restrictions.

God has gifted each of us so that we can bless and edify others. Let's examine the ways our specific gifts can be used to alleviate some of the needs within our families.

Spiritual Gifts

The Bible tells us to build up the body of Christ—the church—through the use of our spiritual gifts. God gives each one of His children a spiritual gift, a special ability to serve and love others. These gifts can also be used to help our relatives in need.

First Corinthians 12:4-7 describes it this way: "There are different kinds of spiritual gifts, but the same Spirit is the source of them all. There are different kinds of service, but we serve the same Lord. God works in different ways, but it is the same God who does the work in all of us. A spiritual gift is given to each of us so we can help each other."

When we exercise our spiritual gifts, we are far less likely to feel burdened, overwhelmed, or burned out in our service. If you've never taken the time to seek out what spiritual gifting you have, start by asking God to reveal the ways in which He has gifted you. You can also ask those around you what gifts they have observed, or you can try exercising a couple of the gifts described in the pages that follow.

A great list to work from is found in Romans 12:4-8:

Just as our bodies have many parts and each part has a
special function, so it is with Christ's body. We are many
parts of one body, and we all belong to each other.

   In his grace, God has given us different gifts for
doing certain things well. So if God has given you
the ability to prophesy, speak out with as much faith
as God has given you. If your gift is serving others,
serve them well. If you are a teacher, teach well. If
your gift is to encourage others, be encouraging. If
it is giving, give generously. If God has given you
leadership ability, take the responsibility seriously.
And if you have a gift for showing kindness to
others, do it gladly.

Kindness

If you have a gift for showing kindness, you excel in understanding a person's emotional needs and quickly discerning
practical ways to minister to that person. When a family first
receives the difficult news of an adverse diagnosis for a loved
one, kindness goes a long way to comfort.

   Even after a family has survived the initial weeks and
months following the diagnosis, someone with the gift of
kindness can be an important confidant and support. After
the shock of a new diagnosis wears off and the delivered
meals from loved ones have ended, family members can continue to provide support.

   Could you offer to care for your loved one's children so
Mom and Dad can have some time together? Ask God to
reveal ways to express your love so that your family members
know they are not alone in their special-needs journey.

Giving

Increased medical needs usually associated with disabilities can adversely affect a family's finances. You may find joy in giving money for a specific need you learn about. You may also use your gift by working with others to meet a need.

However, giving money is not the only way to exercise this spiritual gift. Practical gifts, such as groceries or gift cards, and fun gifts, such as a game the whole family can enjoy, may be just the encouragement your loved ones need.

Encouragement

While each of the spiritual gifts work toward the encouragement of others, a person with the gift of encouragement has a keen sense of what an individual needs to hear to help him or her press on.

If you are gifted in encouragement, then like a cornerman standing just outside the boxing ring or a cheerleader on the sidelines, the words you share with your loved ones will rouse them to keep striving.

A greeting card with kind words or an e-mail reminding that family members are praying can buoy the spirits of a weary mom or dad dealing with the daily struggles of special-needs parenting.

Teaching

Even if you have never stood in front of a classroom, you may still have the gift of teaching. Do you find that people look to you to explain complex ideas in simple, easy-to-understand ways?

For family members affected by disability, your gift of teaching may be useful both when facing inward—within the family—and outward, toward friends and church members. Misconceptions abound in the realm of disability, and you can make a difference by teaching the truth.

Serving

As Joni Eareckson Tada says, "Christians who have the gift of service—they are the ones who often recognize a need before it's articulated."[5] She recalls how Christians with the gift of service ministered to her mother after the diving accident that left her a quadriplegic.

"I remember when two women from my church knocked on our back door, and asked, 'Mrs. Eareckson, we're heading to the market. If you'll give us your shopping list, we'll be happy to pick up the items for you.' My mother was overwhelmed! And she truly appreciated the offer."[6]

If you have the spiritual gift of service, look for the ways your extended family members can use an extra hand. Then ask them if they can use your help in that specific way.

Prophecy

The gift of prophecy has sometimes been called the gift of speaking truth. People with this gift use verses and truths from Scripture to build up and correct those around them.

If you have the gift of prophecy, your marching orders can be taken from 2 Timothy 4:2: "Preach the word of God. Be prepared, whether the time is favorable or not. Patiently correct, rebuke, and encourage your people with good teaching."

While there will certainly be times for you to encourage your loved one or gently challenge damaging assumptions or sinful attitudes, you may find even more opportunities to use your gift to advocate on behalf of your loved ones, proclaiming the truth that every person is created in the image of God.

Leadership

Christians with the gift of leadership learn that the most God-honoring leadership is servant leadership. If you have this gift, you may find yourself organizing other family members to provide respite care or ongoing help.

Or your loved ones who are more closely affected by the disability may benefit from your leadership skills when interfacing with doctors and insurance companies. Be careful to respect boundaries while also letting family members know you are willing to help in this capacity.

Spiritual Gifts at Work

When Eddie and Elena and their three children made a weekend visit to Elena's sister's house, they didn't plan to attend church. They hadn't been to church in over a year. The behavioral challenges of their son Ben were just too complex for their church's children's ministry. Elena's sister, Rachel, knew how much the family needed a time of spiritual refreshment, and her gift of kindness made her want to meet the need.

Rachel brought the problem to her husband, Jon. Having a spiritual gift of leadership, Jon didn't have to think for long: He would watch Ben while his parents went to church. He was already familiar with Ben's special needs, and his nephew would be comfortable with him. They would enjoy each other's company while Eddie and Elena worshiped together for the first time in years.

It wasn't just Eddie and Elena who benefited. Their older son Noah had also missed out on the blessing of church. That

Sunday, his first time in Sunday school in more than a year, the lesson focused on God being ready to help every hour of the day—a specific answer to a question Noah had wondered about earlier that same week.

Rachel and Jon used their spiritual gifts to minister to their family members and meet a tangible need during their visit. Although it was a small sacrifice of time, the significance of the outcome far exceeded their efforts because they had tapped into their God-given gifts to show kindness and lead well.

Above All Else . . . Love

Exercising each of our spiritual gifts provides a powerful opportunity to build up our individual family members and also the entire church. It is important to remember, however, that if we do not practice our spiritual gifts in a spirit of love, they are worthless (see 1 Corinthians 13:1-3).

Maybe you've heard the expression "People don't care how much you know until they know how much you care." For extended family members, this may mean reaching out more often and being consistent so that our loved ones know we genuinely want to help meet their needs. This requires that those directly affected by disability be open and willing to invite others into their sometimes-messy world.

As Laurie Wallin writes, "Someone once put it this way: If you never ask, you never have to hear them say no, but you'll certainly never hear them say yes. So keep asking. Keep inviting. Who knows what joy that could usher into your relationships with your extended family?"[7]

Ask God for discernment in how you can best serve your loved ones in a manner where they experience the love and support of family.

Your Gifted Family Tree

Take time to talk about the spiritual gifts of your loved ones and fill in the boxes on the family tree with names. Who has the gift of giving? Kindness? Serving? Find ways you can acknowledge and celebrate all of the gifts and encourage each person to put his or her gift into service.

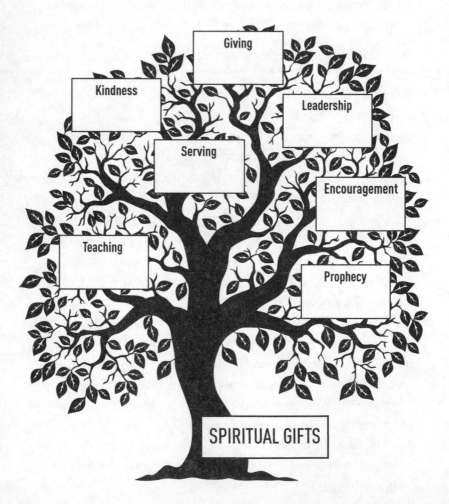

19

Hope, Patience, and Prayer

I yearn for my family to see what makes my son so precious. Everyone notices his challenges, but more than anyone else, family should be able to see what a gift he is.

LENA—MOTHER OF BENJAMIN

❦

EVERYWHERE JOANNA WENT with her daughter Sophie, people tended to ask, "What's wrong with her?" or "How did she get that way?" She understood that their questions were a natural response, but with all the attention, Joanna craved a sense of normalcy and acceptance. Strangers were hard enough to handle, but negative questions from her friends and family often overwhelmed her.

Why couldn't Joanna's family see Sophie's good qualities? Why couldn't they rejoice with her over Sophie's sweet nature and how God seemed to delight in answering her little girl's prayers? Eventually, Joanna found herself wrestling with deep sorrow and questioning what lay ahead for her daughter.

The many ups and downs associated with caring for a loved one with special needs can leave parents and caregivers feeling as if they have nothing left to give. This is where extended family can make a tremendous difference by offering much-needed love and support.

Romans 12:12 is a good family motto: "Rejoice in our confident hope. Be patient in trouble, and keep on praying." When we are certain that God has a place for every family member, we can have hope and stand by one another—accepting and celebrating whatever comes next. We can acknowledge differences and learn to embrace the struggles and grief associated with loss, especially as these relate to individuals with disabilities.

From Celebration to Grief

When Tina's daughter Brianna was born with a disability, Tina's family was supportive beyond expectations. Tina appreciated their help around the house and with Brianna's care, but their attitude weighed on her. Instead of being emotionally supportive of Brianna, she felt her family was making Brianna's disability all about them.

They repeatedly asked, "When is Brianna going to get better? How long until she's normal?" Eventually, Tina couldn't handle their questions and asked them not to come anymore. She didn't realize until much later that she needed to grieve the loss of her dreams for Brianna. All she knew was

There are 6.9 million Americans struggling to care for a loved one with a disability who lives in a faraway location. "Caring from a Distance" is an organization dedicated to serving these long-distance caregivers: www.cfad.org.

that she was not in a good place emotionally and didn't have the energy to take care of her family's need for reassurance.

Tina learned that, yes, we must look for reasons to celebrate and thank God for our loved one's life, but it is also critical to acknowledge our loss and give ourselves permission to grieve.

According to Dr. Mark Baker, it may be one of the best things you can do for your family. He writes, "One of the most important emotions to understand when working with families with special needs is grief. . . . Grieving our losses is a necessary part of growth. In dealing with families with special needs there are often many things to grieve, which is the path to acceptance of the life God has given them."[1]

Whether a disability is the result of an accident, illness, or a congenital condition, the individual and his or her family should expect to grieve.

Dr. Ken Moses, who has dedicated his psychology practice to the needs of families affected by disability, suggests a unique grieving framework that is helpful to these families. Based on his observations, he says the grieving states are "denial, anxiety, fear, guilt, depression, and anger."[2]

He goes on to say that the term *states* is intended to illustrate that grieving does not follow a specified progression. Moses has observed that the resolution of grief for parents with a disabled child is acknowledgment of the loss.[3]

Another important aspect of a family's grief when it comes to disability is to understand that a resolution in one area does not end all sources of grief. Even when parents are able to fully grieve the loss of the dreams they initially had for their child and embrace a new dream, there may be other triggers.

Steve Bundy, whose son Caleb has multiple disabilities, writes, "We remember when children take their first steps, ride a bicycle, graduate from school, start their first career or get married. These rites of passage are considered normal. . . . For families dealing with disability, this can result in . . . despair and hopelessness as they find themselves frozen in one or more stages of life."[4]

Parents may find themselves blindsided by brand-new feelings of grief with each realization that their families may not be able to celebrate these rites of passage with their children with special needs.

Extended family can come alongside loved ones by understanding that even in the midst of rejoicing over the unique individual that God placed in your family, there will be seasons of change and grief. In fact, you, too, may need to go through the hard work of grieving the lost hopes and dreams you imagined for your niece, nephew, cousin, or other family member. Excuse yourself from any feelings of guilt you may have related to grieving. Sorrow is an appropriate response to loss. Be mindful, however, of whether you should express your own emotional struggles with your loved ones. Pray for wisdom, as there is "a time to be quiet and a time to speak" (Ecclesiastes 3:7).

The Ring Theory of Kvetching

In 2013, Susan Silk and Barry Goldman presented an idea they called the "'Ring Theory' of kvetching." This "theory" is intended to help guide people in appropriate interactions with hurting people. To begin with, you create a series of concentric circles, as on an archery target. Then you name the individual who is nearest to the crisis.

As an example, let's use Tina and her daughter, Brianna. You would write Brianna's name in the center circle, as she is the one whose life is most affected by her own disability.

The Impact of Disabilities on Family Life Cycles[5]

Initial Diagnosis: Families are entering a new world, coping with grief stages, informing family and friends, seeking government services, and making ongoing medical decisions.

Childhood and Siblings: Families are adjusting expectations, helping siblings deal with stress, stretching their budgets, and managing special education and therapies.

Transition to Adulthood: Families are assessing levels of independence, seeking vocational and/or residential options, and planning transitions.

Adulthood: Families are managing benefits, changing roles after the loss of parents, reevaluating required services, and facing additional diagnoses with age.

End of Life: Families are seeking moral and ethical guidance for end-of-life decisions, grieving the potentially long "good-bye," and considering life without their loved one.

Next, you would name the people closest to Brianna—her mother Tina, her father, and her siblings—and write their names in the first ring circling Brianna's circle. Then you move outward again, adding extended family members, friends, and acquaintances as you progress outward through the rings.

Once you've labeled your rings, you can apply Silk and Goldman's rule to respond appropriately: comfort in, dump out.

> When you are talking to a person in a ring smaller than yours, someone closer to the center of the crisis, the goal is to help. Listening is often more helpful than talking. But if you're going to open your mouth, ask yourself if what you are about to say is likely to provide comfort and support. If it isn't, don't say it. Don't, for example, give advice. . . . Don't say, "You should hear what happened to me" or "Here's what I would do if I were you." . . .
>
> If you want to scream or cry or complain . . . it's a perfectly normal response. Just do it to someone in a bigger ring.[6]

It is not helpful for you to minimize the grief you feel as a result of your loved one's disability. Nor is it healthy for you to try to "get over it" by comparing what your emotional response is to what you perceive your loved ones are feeling. The guilt brought about by comparisons helps no one. Instead, allow yourself to grieve the loss of your family dream and the hardships your relatives must face. It's okay to grieve alongside your loved ones; just remember to look for emotional support from someone less affected by the crisis.

Supporting through Prayer

No matter how close you are to your loved ones, either physically or relationally, you can always support your family through prayer. God still hears and responds to your prayers even if you feel inadequate to bring your loved one's needs to Him.

Joni Eareckson Tada tells the story of a time when she was preparing to speak at a conference. She noticed she began to get "the sweats," something she has learned indicates that her body is in pain somewhere. She and her assistants hurried to the restroom to try and adjust her sitting position and, while there, met a woman who offered to pray for her.

Immediately, the woman prayed for Joni's body to cool off. Joni confesses, "During her prayer I thought, *But the problem isn't the temperature . . . it's pain.*" Later, however, Joni discovered the sweats had disappeared. She realized God had heard the woman's prayer even though she hadn't known the real source of Joni's sweats.[7]

Just as this woman did not have all of the facts concerning Joni's needs but was still able to pray effectively on her behalf, your prayers can also be effective. Psalm 34:17 says, "The LORD hears his people when they call to him for help." As you come to God on behalf of your family, He will hear your heart's cry.

In some cases, you may lack both information about their needs and any idea of how to pray. If this is the case, take comfort in Luke 4:38 (NIV): "Jesus left the synagogue and went to the home of Simon. Now Simon's mother-in-law was suffering from a high fever, and they asked Jesus to help her." Those who gathered at Simon's house did not make an involved plea; they simply asked Jesus to do something for Simon's mother-in-law. They trusted that Jesus had seen the situation and would be able to help. Likewise, when we are uncertain what to ask for, we can simply ask God to intervene. God hears our requests on behalf of others and answers our prayers even when our best efforts are sorely lacking.

As we continue to pray for our loved ones, we can make our prayers more robust by using Scripture to guide our requests. When we pray this way, we have a unique opportunity to learn what it is that God desires for His children.

For example, 1 Peter 5:7 says, "Give all your worries and cares to God, for he cares about you." Using this verse as a starting point for our prayers for our family, we can pray, "Father in heaven, I ask that You would show Your care to my loved ones. Help them to give You their worries and cares."

As you read Scripture during your own times of study and devotion, God may draw your attention to a wide variety of needs you can address through praying His Word. What follows are some suggested prayers to help you get started.

Scripture-Based Prayers for Your Loved Ones

Prayers for Comfort and Peace

Father in heaven, I ask that You would show Your care to my loved ones. Help them to give You their worries and cares. (See 1 Peter 5:7.)

Lord, please don't let my loved ones fall. Show them that You will take care of them so they will be prompted to give all of their burdens to You. (See Psalm 55:22.)

Father God, You know the health needs of my family. Care for them in their disability as would a nurse; restore health to them. (See Psalm 41:3.)

See also Isaiah 43:1-3.

Prayers for Hope

Lord, give my loved ones a future and a hope. Plan good for them and not disaster. (See Jeremiah 29:11-13.)

God, keep Your promises to my family members. Give them hope they can tightly hold on to. (See Hebrews 10:23.)

Lord God, be kind to my loved ones. Make their suffering be only for a short while, and restore and strengthen them. Support them and place them on a firm foundation. (See 1 Peter 5:10.)

See also Psalm 94:14 and Romans 8:19-21.

Prayers for Wisdom and Direction

Lord, please give my loved ones knowledge of Your will. Increase their spiritual wisdom and understanding. May they continue to grow as they learn to know You better. (See Colossians 1:9-12.)

Lord, enable my family members to trust in You with all their hearts and not to depend on their own understanding. Show them which path to take. (See Proverbs 3:5-6.)

Father God, as You lead my loved ones down a new path, guide them along this unfamiliar way. Brighten the darkness before them and smooth out the road ahead of them. Do not forsake them. (See Isaiah 42:16.)

See also Matthew 11:28-30 and Proverbs 3:13.

Prayers for Unsaved Family

God, be their refuge and strength. Show them that You are always ready to help them in times of trouble. (See Psalm 46:1.)

Father God, please answer them before they even call to you. Before they know to pray to You, while they are still talking about their needs, please won't You go ahead and answer their prayers? (See Isaiah 65:24.)

Lord, please show them that Your name is a strong fortress. May they run to You and find safety. (See Proverbs 18:10.)

See also 2 Thessalonians 3:5 and Ezekiel 11:19-20.

Prayers for Provision

Father God, carry my loved ones in Your arms like a shepherd carries a lamb. Lead them gently as they are absorbed in caring for their young children. Nourish them physically, spiritually, and emotionally. (See Isaiah 40:11.)

Lord, give new strength to my loved ones. Let them not grow weary in what You have given them to do. Let them soar on wings like eagles. (See Isaiah 40:30-31.)

Lord, don't let my loved ones go hungry. Give them every good thing as they trust in You. (See Psalm 34:10.)

See also Philippians 4:19 and Psalm 54:4.

Prayers for Protection

Lord, be a shelter for my loved ones as they are being oppressed by bureaucratic medical systems, unjust social expectations, and ungodly religious rules. Be their refuge in times of trouble. Do not abandon them. (See Psalm 9:9-10.)

God, don't allow the temptations my loved ones face to be more than they can stand. Show them a way out. Be faithful to them. (See 1 Corinthians 10:13.)

Almighty God, give my loved ones rest. Be their refuge and place of safety. Protect them from diseases and disasters. Rescue them and be with them in trouble. Give them Your salvation. (See Psalm 91.)

See also Genesis 28:15 and Exodus 23:20.

Prayers for Courage

Lord, let my loved ones be confident that they will see Your goodness in the midst of the hardships of life. (See Psalm 27:13.)

Father God, may you give my family members confident hope so they will have reason to rejoice. Help them to remember to keep seeking You, and give them patience in the midst of their trouble. (See Romans 12:12.)

Lord God, go ahead of my loved ones. Do not abandon them or fail them. Be near them so that they will not be afraid or panic. Be their Source of strength and courage. (See Deuteronomy 31:6.)

See also Psalm 27:1; Philippians 4:13, 19; and Isaiah 41:10.

A Word about Healing

Just as it is unhelpful to your loved ones for you to fixate on your family member's disability, it is similarly unhelpful for you to insist on praying only for healing. It is certainly not wrong to pray for healing. God may choose to miraculously heal your loved one from his or her disability, but God is much more interested in a deeper healing. He is intent on bringing healing to our souls disabled by sin. Sometimes He uses disability in a family to bring this about.

"God sometimes heals physically, and He is glorified when He does," writes blogger and special-needs mom Kelli Ra Anderson. "But God is also glorified in our weakness. Paul's thorn in the flesh was not removed, despite his prayers, and yet his words fill most of our New Testament and have helped change the course of human history."[8]

Anderson goes on to remind us that God sees us and our loved ones. He knows our times of sorrow and celebration when we need family to gather near. These times of offering emotional and/or spiritual support are an opportunity to honor Him. By looking for ways to support your family and bless their journey with disability, you will showcase God's love and goodness.

Our Family Record of Answered Prayer

In Old Testament times, God's people built stone altars to remind them of God's miraculous answers to prayer. Use this page to record answers to prayer that you can share with your children. This will encourage their faith in a loving God.

Date of Prayer	Person and Need	Bible Promise	Date Answered

20

Become a Disability Advocate

*When my nephew was born with cerebral palsy about four years ago,
my family was in a state of shock. . . . A light bulb goes off when
your life is touched by something such as a disability. . . . You notice
when there's wheelchair access and when there's not. . . . Because
I was in a situation where it wasn't my child . . . I could actually
spend more time and energy on advocating issues.*

CHERYL HINES—ACTRESS, AUNT, AND ADVOCATE FOR PEOPLE
WITH CEREBRAL PALSY

❦

WHILE WE TYPICALLY think of advocacy as the role of an
attorney or a professional intermediary, there are plenty of
life-giving ways you can support a family member with a
disability. In general, all parents are advocates for their children's
well-being, but parents of children with special needs
quickly learn the importance of advocating for the physical,
emotional, and educational services their children require.
In her book *Different Dream Parenting: A Practical Guide to
Raising a Child with Special Needs*, Jolene Philo describes the
transition parents of special-needs children make when they
first become aware that something in their child's development
is not typical. Addressing parents, she writes,

REAL FAMILIES, REAL NEEDS

Advocates speak on behalf of those who lack the ability to speak for themselves. They use their strengths to champion the rights of the powerless. Which sounds a whole lot like what parents typically do for their kids. . . . But as a parent ambushed by a diagnosis, your advocacy duties are out of the ordinary, and your season of advocacy may be longer, more complex, and filled with unexpected challenges.[1]

As parents advocate in every sphere of their child's life, they face extraordinary demands. There are medical appointments, therapy sessions, classroom adaptations, and church programs—just to name a few. Exhausted parents can benefit from extended family members who are willing to provide additional support. Some parents have even noticed that advocates other than themselves are listened to more carefully. In that situation, your efforts to show up and talk on behalf of a child's needs can speak volumes.

> **The good news is that the only "special knowledge" you need is that your loved one deserves respect and consideration.**

Perhaps you think, *That may work for someone else, but I don't have any special knowledge about education or health concerns. I don't have any expertise to draw on in an advocacy situation.* The good news is that the only "special knowledge" you need is that your loved one deserves respect and consideration. Many times, all that is required is to pay attention and ask good questions.

Dr. Jeff McNair, director of church relations for the

Christian Institute on Disability at Joni and Friends, works to be an active advocate for his friends with disabilities. On his blog *Disabled Christianity*, he tells of one such time:

> I was recently at an individualized education program (IEP) meeting for a young girl with down syndrome. By law, the education of persons receiving special education is to be individualized partially because these individuals have demonstrated [they] have difficulty being successful under the regular curriculum and also because oftentimes very specialized approaches are necessary. Anyway, in this meeting diagnostic information was shared about the girl. The teacher indicated that the student only knew about 10 letters of the alphabet (although at the meeting she wasn't sure which those were) and could barely write her name. However, the objective for the IEP was that the student would remember to place spaces between words when she is copying a paragraph from the blackboard. OK, so the most important thing (among others which made their way into the education plan) was that a girl who didn't know letters would successfully place spaces between words in a copied paragraph. Does this strike you as somewhat silly? Even the parents, two intelligent people, didn't speak up about the objective at the meeting until I spoke up.[2]

In saying this, Dr. McNair is not dismissing the role of the parents in advocating for their daughter. He is simply showing that in the cloud of difficult decision-making, even well-meaning systems and individuals can fail to adequately see what's best for the person with a disability. When a child with a disability has additional friends and family looking out for his or her needs, he or she is more likely to receive the best care possible. Your presence can help make that happen.

Love in Action

Children and their parents are not the only individuals who can benefit from additional advocacy on the part of extended family members. Adults with disabilities often need strong advocates as well. In the same blog post, McNair gives another example of when a woman with a mild-to-moderate intellectual disability needed an advocate. We'll call her Martha.

> [Martha] was living on her own in an apartment
> with about 3 cats. . . . The landlord of the complex
> decided that pets would no longer be permitted in
> the complex. Tenants were given two months to
> get rid of their pets. . . . [Martha] insisted that she
> wouldn't get rid of her cats. When case workers
> from the state attempted to help her to even discuss
> the possibility, she became verbally abusive. At that
> point the case workers no longer attempted to work
> with [Martha] to get rid of her cats.[3]

McNair then spells out the consequences of this stalemate between Martha and her caseworkers. After nearly ten years of independent living, Martha's refusal to get rid of her cats caused her to be evicted. Once evicted, she no longer qualified for rent assistance from the government, so she could not afford to live in her own apartment. Without the ability to live on her own, Martha had no place to live but in a group home designed for people with fewer independent living skills. In this group home, she not only had less freedom but also fewer opportunities to exercise the skills that had taken years of work to establish.

This scenario could have been different if Martha had a cousin, aunt, or other loved one to come alongside her. What if a cousin had found a family member willing to take the cats where they could be visited regularly? What if an aunt had been able to help her caseworkers better empathize with her frustration and grief over losing her feline friends? What if family had persisted in helping her work through the stressful change? Any of these interventions could have allowed Martha to enjoy many more years of independent living.

Third-Party Advocacy

Shannon Dingle passionately advocated for children with disabilities through many years of service to her church community before her own family benefited from the church's disability ministry.

One day she realized that she was a more assertive advocate for children in the church than she was for her own family. At that point, she sought someone who could fill the role of an effective third-party advocate.[4]

You may find this to be true for your own loved ones. As a third-party advocate, you may be skilled at note taking in the doctor's office, keeping track of what is recommended, and bringing up inconsistencies in care. Or perhaps you can best help by shepherding insurance claims through the bureaucratic maze. Whatever situations your loved ones face, they may greatly benefit from your support.

In the midst of your advocacy on behalf of family members, you may uncover entire populations who need someone to speak up for them. The Crosier family was stunned and grieved to discover that their three-month-old son, Simon, died because a doctor placed a DNR (Do Not Resuscitate) order on his medical file. They had no idea that it was possible for doctors to do so without parental permission. As a result, Simon's family and relatives have worked to make this practice illegal in the state of Kansas.[5] Their advocacy now has the potential to save the lives of other children.

Advocacy through Awareness

Naomi Ruperto was diagnosed with Type 1 diabetes as a preteen. Now a young adult, she invites her friends and family to join her each year for the Juvenile Diabetes Research Foundation fund-raising walk.

Having them by her side to encourage her and keep her company while she walks serves to remind her of their support throughout her management of diabetes. The annual walk has become a highlight because of how much she is encouraged when the people she loves donate their time and resources, demonstrating how much they care.

You may be surprised at how much your participation in awareness events or research fund-raisers will mean to your loved ones. Is there an awareness walk for the specific disability or syndrome your loved one lives with? Is there a fund-raising drive for researching a cure? What about volunteering at a local Special Olympics game day? When you prioritize your participation in disability awareness events, you make disability more known in your community, and through this, you are advocating on behalf of your loved ones.

Advocacy through Affirmation

Another way to advocate for loved ones with disabilities is to affirm the value of their sufferings.

Joan's mother-in-law suffered a stroke, and her health quickly deteriorated. Everyone in the family braced themselves for her death . . . but it didn't come. Instead, their loved one lingered for weeks, then months, in pain. To Joan, it all seemed pointless. God could not have any reason for letting her mother-in-law continue on in pain, could He? Wouldn't it just be better to let her die quickly?

In a 2007 radio broadcast, Joni Eareckson Tada addressed the tragedy of "right to die" laws. Over a ten-year period in Oregon, following the passing of its "death with dignity" law, the percentage of people choosing death through lethal prescription stayed about the same, at one tenth of one percent of the population. During that same time period, hospice care rates increased significantly.

"These statistics are so revealing, because it proves that people with terminal illnesses really don't want to die—what they want is relief from pain. They want help, they want comfort, they don't want to be alone. That's what this report reveals," Joni concluded.[6]

Part of your advocacy for your loved one must include promoting the idea that his or her life has value, regardless of the disability. If God has chosen not to end an individual's suffering on earth, then He has a good purpose for it. Whether we can see any earthly gain for a person continuing on when severely disabled, there is an eternal good that God is working toward. As 2 Peter 3:8 says, each day is filled with "a thousand years" of moments God can use for His purpose.

Church Family

For many families that have children involved in the disability ministry programs at church, their church members become like extended family. Times of rest are provided through church-sponsored respite events, they have somewhere to turn for babysitting needs or when emergencies arise, and they may feel a sense of love and understanding that's found nowhere else.

Some churches have recognized the void in care and have created nonprofit service organizations to help meet the needs historically met by extended family members. Mosaic Church of Central Arkansas established Vine and Village. One of the main programs, which ministers to adults with disabilities, is called Extended Family. Through Extended Family, volunteers celebrate birthdays and holidays, provide transportation for medical appointments, build relationships, and offer other services that were once expected of extended family.

The services these church volunteers and program managers provide meet a critical need. For more than three and a half decades, Joni and Friends has worked to train and equip churches to be effective in disability ministry. In recent years, there has been a steadily growing movement worldwide among churches. This intentionality is exciting and long overdue. But a problem remains: Churches cannot meet every need.

In the first century, the church in Ephesus faced a similar problem. Many widows relied on the church to provide for them, as they had no way of earning an income. The apostle Paul agreed that it was the church's job to help care for these widows, but he understood it was also a large burden for some churches to bear. So Paul instructed Timothy to set standards requiring those widows with relatives in the church to be cared for by their own family. "If a woman who is a believer has relatives who are widows, she must take care of them and not put the responsibility on the church. Then the church can care for the widows who are truly alone."[7]

In the same way, even wealthy churches with vibrant disability ministries can be overwhelmed by the needs of families in their community. Jill's House, an overnight respite service birthed out of McLean Bible Church, has such a lengthy wait-list that they suggest interested families register their child with special needs six months before the child is even old enough to participate.[8]

You may be panicking now, wanting to point out that you don't have a nursing degree or experience in special education. How can you be expected to take on the responsibility of caring for your loved one? The good news is that you can start small.

Dave knew his sister and brother-in-law could use help, but he didn't have the faintest idea of how he would manage the care of his niece Hannah. Even the idea of being left alone with her for a few minutes overwhelmed him. How could he be of any use to his sister?

Finally, Dave had an idea. He signed Hannah up for a respite event at his church, and he volunteered to be her buddy. He listened attentively during the volunteer training before the event and took mental notes throughout the evening.

As he spent time with Hannah in the structured environment of the church-sponsored respite event, he gained confidence in his ability to provide the attention she needed. After the event, he felt prepared to give his sister and brother-in-law other breaks without the help of his church.

If you are not aware of a local church providing respite events or other outreach to families affected by disability, don't despair! There are plenty of other opportunities for you to learn how to provide the support your loved ones need. Ultimately, the best place to start is by simply being a part of your loved one's life.

Clarissa remembers a pivotal experience with her brother: "A couple of years ago we went to an amusement park with my family, and I asked my brother to help our son in the bathroom. I couldn't go because they didn't have a family restroom. My brother's eyes got really big. It finally clicked for him that this is what normal life is for us. Later he made a huge effort to make it to a party we had in my son's honor. His intentionality meant so much to us."

At the root of all advocacy efforts is someone who cares enough to make a sacrifice—to learn more, to show up, and to speak up. In 1 John 2:1, we see how much our heavenly Father cares for each of us in our weakness. Jesus is called our Advocate because He stands up for us when we are helpless and because He made the ultimate sacrifice. Pray about how God might be calling you to advocate on behalf of extended family. What are you willing to sacrifice? What will be the fruit of your family tree (see Jeremiah 17:8)?

Host a Video and Popcorn Night

Everyone loves a family night at the movies. Below we've listed four twenty-eight-minute videos that can help you start new discussions on what it means to be a friend and advocate for adults and children with disabilities.

Joni and Friends television programs are hosted by Joni Eareckson Tada, who highlights a refreshingly honest approach to people's toughest questions about the goodness of God in a world shattered by pain and suffering. After each episode, ask family members these key questions:

- What did the person with a disability need most in life?
- Who came alongside to meet that need?
- What changed for those who needed support?
- What changed for those who gave their support?

Joni and Friends Family Retreat: Short-Term Missionaries
www.joniandfriends.org/television/joni-and
-friends-family-retreat

For parents of a child with special needs, the extra challenges of daily life can be exhausting. At a Joni and Friends Family Retreat, a volunteer Short-Term Missionary is paired with each family to make sure parents get a much-needed break. Share a week with four Short-Term Missionaries as they step out of their comfort zones and into the world of a child with special needs. Through this unique opportunity for service and friendship, families and volunteers experience God's love in a whole new way.

Mark and David: Unconditional Friends
www.joniandfriends.org/television/mark-david
-unconditional-friends

This inside look at the lives of two adult men with intellectual disabilities (one single and one married) includes comments from Dr. Jeff McNair, director of church relations at Joni and Friends and professor of education and disability studies at California Baptist University. Viewers will gain new insights into the challenges faced by adults with intellectual disabilities living in our communities and the limitations placed on them from cultural misunderstanding and perception.

Christian Royal: In the Potter's Hands

www.joniandfriends.org/television/christian-royal -potters-hands

When Christian Royal's parents were told "Your son can't be educated," they refused to be discouraged. Instead, they persisted in helping their son find a path that has led to purpose and joy in his life. This is a remarkable story of how a young man with Down syndrome found not only a skill he loves to do but also one in which he excels far beyond what most people can achieve. And the result? A higher level of confidence, a thriving business, and a special niche in his community. Can those who are profoundly disabled learn? Watch and see.

Sarah and Lydia: Friends Forever

www.joniandfriends.org/television/sarah-lydia -friends-forever

Sarah Kritikos was lonely. With multiple disabilities and medical issues, she wondered if she would ever have a true friend. Meeting Lydia Abell at a Joni and Friends Family Retreat was the answer to Sarah's prayer. Lydia doesn't have a disability, but from the moment she met Sarah, she knew the Lord had formed a bond between them and filled a vacancy in both of their hearts. This heartwarming story is reassurance that God knows our hearts' desires, and that every one of His children has a place in the body of Christ.

Beyond Suffering Resources

Beyond Suffering®: A Christian View on Disability Ministry

Study Guide by Joni Eareckson Tada and Steve Bundy with Pat Verbal
Leader's Guide by Joni Eareckson Tada and Kathy McReynolds

This groundbreaking course of study will transform the way Christians view God's plan for disability and suffering. The curriculum contains 16 lessons organized into four modules:

- Overview of Disability Ministry
- Theology of Suffering and Disability
- The Church and Disability Ministry
- Introduction to Bioethics

Beyond Suffering Study Guide
291 pages with CD-Rom
ISBN 978-0-9838484-0-0

Beyond Suffering Leader's Guide
1 CD-Rom, 2 DVDs
ISBN 978-0-9838484-1-7

Each module is designed to give Christians a solid understanding of the main issues involved in various aspects of disability ministry. Students who embrace this study will gain a sense of confidence in knowing that they are part of a movement that God is orchestrating to fulfill his command in Luke 14:21: "Go out quickly into the streets and alleys of the town and bring in the poor, the crippled, the blind, and the lame."

Also Available in Braille, Spanish, and iBook Editions

Beyond Suffering Braille Edition
Study Guide, Course Reader & Leader's
Manual in a .brf format for use with
Braille reading software and printers
ISBN 978-0-9838484-4-8

Beyond Suffering Bible
The *Beyond Suffering Bible* is the first Bible
to directly address those who suffer and the
people who love and care for them.
ISBN 978-1-4143-9202-8

Beyond Suffering iBook Edition
The downloadable, fully-interactive version
of the Study Guide and Leader's Guide for
use on iPad comes alive with additional
photos, videos and graphics to inspire the
21st century student. Available on iTunes.
ISBN 978-0-9838484-5-5

http://www.joniandfriends.org/real-families-real-needs
P.O. Box 3333, Agoura Hills, CA 91376
818-707-5664 • TTY:818-707-9707

and Friends

Christian Institute on Disability

More about Joni and Friends

The Mission of Joni and Friends Is . . .

to communicate the gospel and equip Christ-honoring churches worldwide to evangelize and disciple people affected by disabilities. Founded by Joni Eareckson Tada, a quadriplegic since 1967, Joni and Friends is committed to advancing disability ministry around the world. The Joni and Friends International Disability Center in Agoura Hills, California, is the hub of this ministry that annually reaches thousands of families by presenting the gospel of Jesus Christ and training, discipling, and mentoring people to use their spiritual gifts.

Joni and Friends Christian Institute on Disability . . .

was established in 2007 to advance the important work of disability education by aggressively promoting a biblical worldview and life-giving truth on issues pertaining to life, dignity, justice, and equality that affect people with disabilities. This is carried out through leadership development, reflection on ethical questions, and advocacy in churches, colleges, and seminaries worldwide. Learn more at www .joniandfriends.org.

Authors and Contributors

Authors

Joni Eareckson Tada, founder and CEO of Joni and Friends, is an international advocate for people with disabilities. Joni became a quadriplegic following an accident in 1967. She is an artist and an author of numerous bestselling books, including *Joni & Ken: An Untold Love Story, Life in the Balance, Beside Bethesda,* and *Beyond Suffering: A Christian View on Disability Ministry,* and served as executive editor of the *Beyond Suffering Bible.* She and her husband, Ken, reside in Calabasas, California.

    Steve Bundy, senior vice president of integration at Joni and Friends, is a pastor, speaker, and published author. Steve coauthored *Another Kind of Courage: God's Design for Fathers of Families Affected by Disability* and *Life in the Balance* and was an executive editor of the *Beyond Suffering Bible.* He was also coexecutive producer of the Telly Award–winning television series *Making Sense of Autism.* Steve lives in California with his wife, Melissa, and two sons.

    Pat Verbal is an author who shares from her twenty-five years of experience as an associate pastor and educator. Her books include *Special Needs Ministry for Children, Special*

Needs Smart Pages, *Life in the Balance*, and *Beyond Suffering: A Christian View on Disability Ministry*. Pat is senior manager of publishing and ministry resources at Joni and Friends and holds an MA in pastoral studies. Inspired by the courage of her late husband's suffering, she served as managing editor/contributor for the *Beyond Suffering Bible*.

Contributors

Anna Brady, MSEd, is a doctoral candidate in the disability disciplines PhD program at Utah State University and has two brothers with disabilities.

Cavin Harper is the founder and executive director of the Christian Grandparenting Network (www .ChristianGrandparenting.net) and the author of *Courageous Grandparenting: Unshakable Faith in a Broken World*.

Rebecca A. C. Olson is a contributing author to *Life in the Balance Leader's Guide* and the *Beyond Suffering Bible* as well as a contributing editor to *Beyond Suffering: A Christian View on Disability Ministry*.

Chonda Ralston MA, has served as an editor and contributor for numerous Joni and Friends resources, including *Life in the Balance*, *Beyond Suffering: A Christian View on Disability Ministry*, and the *Beyond Suffering Bible*.

Notes

CHAPTER 1—COURAGE UNDER PRESSURE

1. Joni Eareckson Tada, "Notice the Me's," *More Precious Than Silver: 366 Daily Devotional Readings* (Grand Rapids, MI: Zondervan, 1998), March 24.
2. See Romans 8:15.
3. Steve Bundy, "Does My Son Need to Be Healed?" in Joni Eareckson Tada and Steve Bundy with Pat Verbal, *Beyond Suffering Study Guide: A Christian View on Disability Ministry* (Agoura Hills, CA: Joni and Friends, 2012), 2–3.
4. This is not to suggest, of course, that physical healings have not occurred, nor that physical healings do not lead to people finding Christ.
5. Bundy, 4–5.
6. Joni Eareckson Tada and Dave and Jan Dravecky, eds., *The Encouragement Bible: The Answer for Those Who Hurt, NIV* (Grand Rapids, MI: Zondervan Publishing House, 2001), 1409.

CHAPTER 2—COURAGE TO SURRENDER YOUR FAMILY TO GOD

1. Merriam-Webster, accessed May 14, 2017, http://www.merriam-webster .com/dictionary, s. vv. "defeat," "surrender."
2. See 1 John 1:9.

CHAPTER 3—COURAGE TO STAND AS BROTHERS

1. Jacquie Goetz Bluethmann, "Dads Dealing with a Special Needs Diagnosis in Their Kids," *Metro Parent for Southeast Michigan*, December 19, 2011, http://www.metroparent.com/daily/parenting/special-needs-resources /dads-dealing-with-a-special-needs-diagnosis-in-their-kids/.
2. Ibid.
3. David Lyons and Linda Lyons Richardson, *Don't Waste the Pain: Learning*

to Grow through Suffering (Colorado Springs: NavPress, 2010), 239. Used by permission. All rights reserved. https://www.navpress.com/.

4. Ibid., 243.
5. See Psalm 119:11.
6. See Hebrews 4:16 and Psalm 68:35.
7. See Hebrews 10:23-25.
8. Dave Deuel, "Outreach and In-Reach to Families Affected by Disabilities: Ministering through Family Groups," in Joni Eareckson Tada and Steve Bundy with Pat Verbal, *Beyond Suffering Study Guide: A Christian View on Disability Ministry* (Agoura Hills, CA: Joni and Friends, 2012), 1–2.
9. Washington State Fathers Network, accessed May 19, 2017, https://fathersnetwork.org/.
10. *Connections*, Winter 2013, 10, http://fathersnetwork.org/wp-content/uploads/2013/04/Connections-Winter-2013-Final.pdf.
11. Dietrich Bonhoeffer, *Life Together: A Discussion of Christian Fellowship* (New York: Harper & Row, 1954), 100. See also Goodreads, accessed May 19, 2017, http://www.goodreads.com/quotes/688594-the-christian-however-must-bear-the-burden-of-a-brother.
12. Josh McDowell, *The Father Connection: How You Can Make the Difference in Your Child's Self-Esteem and Sense of Purpose* (Nashville: B&H Publishing Group, 2008), 7.

CHAPTER 4—COURAGE TO TRUST IN GOD'S ETERNAL PLAN

1. Jerry Bridges, *Trusting God* (Colorado Springs: NavPress, 2008), ix.
2. Ibid., 4
3. David Lyons and Linda Lyons Richardson, *Don't Waste the Pain: Learning to Grow Through Suffering* (Colorado Springs: NavPress, 2010), 162–63. Used by permission. All rights reserved. https://www.navpress.com/.
4. Ibid.
5. "The Problem of Evil and Suffering in Our World," in Joni Eareckson Tada and Steve Bundy with Pat Verbal, *Beyond Suffering Study Guide: A Christian View on Disability Ministry* (Agoura Hills, CA: Joni and Friends, 2012), 6–7.
6. See Nathaniel's Hope, http://www.nathanielshope.org.
7. See Special Needs Alliance, http://www.specialneedsalliance.org.
8. Billy Graham, *Nearing Home: Life, Faith, and Finishing Well* (Nashville: Thomas Nelson, 2011), 166–67.

CHAPTER 5—A TROUBLED HEART: EMBRACING YOUR CHILD'S DIAGNOSIS

1. Kristin Reinsberg, MS, LMFT, "States of Grief for Parents of Children with Special Needs," AbilityPath.org, October 20, 2015, http://abilitypath.org/2015/10/20/states-of-grief/.
2. Ellen Stumbo, "Dear Mom Dealing with Your Child's New Diagnosis,"

Ellen Stumbo (blog), http://www.ellenstumbo
.com/dear-mom-dealing-childs-new-diagnosis.

3. Philip Yancey, *Where Is God When It Hurts?* (Grand Rapids, MI: Zondervan, 2002), 198.

4. Jerry Sittser, *A Grace Revealed: How God Redeems the Story of Your Life* (Grand Rapids, MI: Zondervan, 2012), 19.

5. Susan W. Enouen, PE, "Down Syndrome and Abortion," Life Issues Institue, Inc., Januray 1, 2007, http://www.lifeissues.org/2007/01/down-syndrome-abortion/.

6. Philip Yancey, *Reaching for the Invisible God* (Grand Rapids, MI: Zondervan, 2000), 181.

CHAPTER 6—A JOYFUL HEART: BECOMING YOUR CHILD'S
BIGGEST FAN

1. Used with permission. Based on submission from Debbie Salter Goodwin, http://www.debbiegoodwin.net.

2. Laurie Wallin, *Get Your Joy Back: Banishing Resentment and Reclaiming Confidence in Your Special Needs Family* (Grand Rapids, MI: Kregel, 2015), 18.

3. Kay Warren, *Choose Joy: Because Happiness Isn't Enough* (Grand Rapids, MI: Revell, 2012), 193.

4. Andrew and Rachel Wilson, *The Life We Never Expected: Hopeful Reflections on the Challenges of Parenting Children with Special Needs* (Wheaton, IL: Crossway, 2016), 147–48.

5. Kaylee Page, "(in)couragement for (in)ablers," *Apple Pie, Anyone?* (blog), November 21, 2012 (guest blogger), https://texasnorth.wordpress.com/2012/11/21/incouragement-for-inablers-4/.

6. Used with permission. Based on submission from Gillian Marchenko, http://www.gillianmarchenko.com.

7. Used with permission. Based on submission from Sandi Anderson, http://www.joelsvisionarts.com.

8. Warren, 163.

9. See giant-sequoia.com, accessed May 23, 2017, https://www.giant-sequoia.com/faqs/giant-sequoia-questions/.

CHAPTER 7—A NURTURING HEART: KEEPING MARRIAGE AND
FAMILY UNITED

1. Used with permission. Based on submission from Melissa Bundy.

2. Laura E. Marshak, PhD, and Fran Pollock Prezant, MEd, CCC-SLP, *Married with Special-Needs Children: A Couples' Guide to Keeping Connected* (Bethesda, MD: Woodbine, 2007), 5.

3. Joe and Cindi Ferrini, "Special Needs and Marriage," Focus on the Family, accessed May 23, 2017, https://www.focusonthefamily.com/marriage/marriage-challenges/special-needs-and-marriage/special-needs-and-marriage.

4. Joe and Cindi Ferrini, "Stress and Conflict," Focus on the Family, accessed May 23, 2017, https://www.focusonthefamily.com/marriage/marriage -challenges/special-needs-and-marriage/stress-and-conflict.

5. John Piper, *This Momentary Marriage: A Parable of Permanence* (Wheaton, IL: Crossway, 2012), 97.

6. Ibid., 101.

7. "5 Tips for Couples Parenting a Special Needs Child," Enabled Kids, October 14, 2013, http://enabledkids.ca/coping-as-a-couple-while -parenting-a-child-with-special-needs/.

8. Gary Chapman, *The Five Love Languages: The Secret to Love That Lasts* (Chicago: Northfield Publishing, 2015), 22.

9. Ibid., 142.

10. Steve Bundy, interview on "Making Sense of Autism: Part 2—Truth for the Church," Joni and Friends Television Series, episode 31, season 2, http:// www.joniandfriends.org/television/making-sense-autism-part-2/.

CHAPTER 8—A TRUSTING HEART: SHARING CHRIST WHEN SETBACKS COME

1. Used with permission. Based on submission from Kathy Kuhl.

2. Sarah Parshall Perry, "Invisible Diagnoses and the God Who Sees," *Not Alone: Finding Faith and Friendship for the Special-Needs Journey* (blog), December 1, 2015, http://specialneedsparenting.net/invisible-2.

3. Kathy Kuhl, "Help Your Child Defeat Discouragement: Encouraging Your Child series, Part 1," *Learn Differently* (blog), August 27, 2014, http://www .learndifferently.com/2014/08/27/help-your-child-defeat-discouragement/.

4. Cassandra, "Letting Go Without Letting Go," accessed July 2016, http:// chosenfamilies.org/2014/01/letting-go-without-letting-go/.

5. Avery T. Willis Jr. and Matt Willis, *Learning to Soar: How to Grow through Transitions and Trials* (Colorado Springs: NavPress, 2009), 78.

CHAPTER 9—REALITIES FOR SIBLINGS

1. See Sibling Support Project, https://www.siblingsupport.org/.

2. Don Meyer and Emily Holl, eds., *The Sibling Survival Guide: Indispensable Information for Brothers and Sisters of Adults With Disabilities* (Bethesda, MD: Woodbine House, 2014), 6.

3. Joni Eareckson Tada, "Siblings and Disabilities," Joni and Friends Radio broadcast, Feb. 5, 2015, http://www.joniandfriends.org/radio/1-minute /siblings-and-disabilities/.

4. Sandra Peoples, "Advice on How to Encourage Special-Needs Siblings (From a Special-Needs Sibling)," Key Ministry, *Special Needs Parenting* (blog), July 18, 2016, http://www.keyministry.org /specialneedsparenting/2016/7/18/advice-on-how-to-encourage-special -needs-siblings-from-a-special-needs-sibling.

5. Joni Eareckson Tada, "A Sister's Role," Joni and Friends Radio broadcast, May 27, 2013, http://www.joniandfriends.org/radio/1-minute/sisters-role/.
6. Paul W. Power, ScD, and Arthur E. Dell Orto, PhD, *The Resilient Family: Living with Your Child's Illness or Disability* (Notre Dame, IN: Sorin Books, 2003), 132.
7. See Sibling Leadership Network, http://siblingleadership.org.

CHAPTER 10—GROWING UP TOO FAST
1. Don Meyer, "Always Secure Your Own Oxygen Mask Before Assisting Others," in *The Sibling Survival Guide*, eds. Don Meyer and Emily Holl (Bethesda, MD: Woodbine House, 2014), 73–91.
2. "Brothers and Sisters" (online documentary), Attitude, May 22, 2011, http://attitudelive.com/watch/Brothers-and-Sisters.
3. Find local respite care workers at the ARCH National Respite Network's website: http://archrespite.org.
4. See http://www.joniandfriends.org/family-retreats/.
5. "Soeren Palumbo Illinois Senate Address 5/16/07," YouTube video, posted by Drew Palumbo, May 28, 2007, https://www.youtube.com/watch?v=b9ut2feg2GU.
6. See Matthew 10:30.
7. See Psalm 139:13-16.
8. Peter Schuntermann, "The Sibling Experience: Growing Up with a Child Who Has Pervasive Developmental Disorder or Mental Retardation," *Harvard Review of Psychiatry* 15, no. 3 (May/June 2007): 93–108, doi: 10.1080/10673220701432188.

CHAPTER 11—IMPROVING COMMUNICATION
1. Kristen McCullough and Shirley R. Simon, "Feeling Heard: A Support Group for Siblings of Children with Developmental Disabilities," *Social Work with Groups*, 34, no. 3-4 (July 2011): 320–29, doi: 10.1080/01609513.2011.558819.
2. Alicia Arenas, "TEDxSanAntonio—Alicia Arenas—Recognizing Glass Children," YouTube video of TED Talk, posted by TEDx Talks, December 27, 2010, https://www.youtube.com/watch?v=MSwqo-g2Tbk.
3. See Romans 12:4-5; 1 Corinthians 12:12-27; Ephesians 4:1-16; Hebrews 10:24-25.
4. See Sibling Leadership Network, http://siblingleadership.org.
5. See Sibling Support Project, https://www.siblingsupport.org.

CHAPTER 12—HELPING SIBLINGS CONNECT
1. T. Moyson and H. Roeyers, "'The Overall Quality of My Life as a Sibling Is All Right, But of Course, It Could Always Be Better.' Quality of life of siblings of children with intellectual disability: the siblings' perspectives," *Journal of Intellectual Disability Research* 56, no. 1 (January 2012): 87–101, doi: 10.1111/j.1365-2788.2011.01393.x.

2. Kristen McCullough and Shirley R. Simon, "Feeling Heard: A Support Group for Siblings of Children with Developmental Disabilities," *Social Work with Groups* 34, no. 3-4 (2011): 320–29, doi: 10.1080/01609513.2011.558819.
3. For more help with siblings, visit http://siblingleadership.org/.
4. See Romans 8:28.

CHAPTER 13—MY GRANDCHILD HAS A DISABILITY—NOW WHAT?
1. Lon Adams, "Diagnosis Issues with Lon Adams," Need Project, podcast audio, March 14, 2008, http://www.needproject.org/~need06/index.php/podcasts/204-diagnosis-issues-with-lon-adams.

CHAPTER 14—SUPPORTING YOUR GRANDCHILD
1. "CASK-Related Intellectual Disability," U. S. National Library of Medicine, Genetics Home Reference, accessed May 28, 2017, https://ghr.nlm.nih.gov/condition/cask-related-intellectual-disability.
2. 2 Corinthians 5:18.
3. K. Kuhlthau, K. S. Hill, R. Yucel, and J. M. Perrin, "Financial Burden for Families of Children with Special Health Care Needs," *Maternal and Child Health Journal* 9, no. 2 (June 2005), 207–18: doi: 10.1007/s10995-005-4870-x, abstract available at https://www.ncbi.nlm.nih.gov/pubmed/15965627.
4. For more information on special-needs trusts, see Special Needs Alliance, http://www.specialneedsalliance.org. Be sure to seek legal advice, preferably from a lawyer who specializes in special-needs trusts.

CHAPTER 15—HUGE INVESTMETS, HUGE REWARDS
1. See Philippians 4:19.
2. See Joshua 3.

CHAPTER 16—BUILDING A GODLY HERITAGE
1. Robert Frank, "Millionaire Kids to Inherit Most of Their Parents' Fortunes," CNBC, May 6, 2015, http://www.cnbc.com/2015/05/06/millionaire-kids-to-inherit-most-of-their-parents-fortunes.html.
2. See Philippians 4:19.
3. See Psalm 50:10.
4. See Christian Grandparenting Network, https://www.christiangrandparenting.net/.

CHAPTER 17—ACCEPTANCE AND INCLUSION
1. Barb Dittrich, "7 Tips for Summer Gatherings When You Include Special-Needs Families," Key Ministry, *Special Needs Parenting* (blog), July 13, 2016, http://www.keyministry.org/specialneedsparenting/2016/7/13/7-tips-for-summer-gatherings-when-you-include-special-needs-families.

2. Adapted from Joni and Friends, "Party Strategies for People with Disabilities," DisabilityCampaign.org, accessed May 30, 2017, http://disabilitycampaign.org/media/filer_public/88/2b/882be12d-6751-487f-bfde-eddc1fd502e0/party-strategies-for-people-with-disabilities.pdf.
3. Joni Eareckson Tada, "Dying Together," Joni and Friends Radio broadcast, November 24, 2009, http://www.joniandfriends.org/radio/5-minute/dying-together.
4. See Joni Eareckson Tada and Steve Bundy with Pat Verbal, *Beyond Suffering Study Guide: A Christian View on Disability Ministry* (Agoura Hills, CA: Joni and Friends, 2012).
5. Merriam-Webster, accessed May 30, 2017, http://www.merriam-webster.com/dictionary, s. v."handicap."
6. Ellen Stumbo, "Why Are We So Afraid of Disability?" Key Ministry, *Special Needs Parenting* (blog), July 12, 2016, http://www.keyministry.org/specialneedsparenting/2016/7/12/why-are-we-so-afraid-of-disability?rq=acceptance.
7. Adapted from "Helpful Hints," Easterseals, accessed May 30, 2017, http://www.easterseals.com/explore-resources/facts-about-disability/helpful-hints.html.

CHAPTER 18—STANDING IN THE GAP
1. See Ruth 3:10.
2. See Ruth 4:15.
3. See Esther 2:5-4:17.
4. Laurie Wallin, *Get Your Joy Back: Banishing Resentment and Reclaiming Confidence in Your Special Needs Family* (Grand Rapids, MI: Kregel, 2015), 88.
5. Joni Eareckson Tada, *Christianity with Its Sleeves Rolled Up* (Agoura Hills, CA: Joni and Friends, 2017), 7.
6. Ibid., 5.
7. Wallin, 94.

CHAPTER 19—HOPE, PATIENCE, AND PRAYER
1. Mark W. Baker, "Dealing with the Emotions of Those with Special Needs," in Joni Eareckson Tada and Steve Bundy with Pat Verbal, *Beyond Suffering Study Guide: A Christian View on Disability Ministry* (Agoura Hills, CA: Joni and Friends, 2012), n.p.
2. Ken Moses, PhD, "The Impact of Childhood Disability: The Parent's Struggle," PENT Forum, 2004, http://www.pent.ca.gov/beh/dis/parentstruggle_DK.pdf.
3. Ibid.
4. Steve Bundy, "What Is Life Like for People with Disabilities?" in *Designed by God: A Biblical Theology of Disability, Suffering and Church Ministry* (Agoura Hills, CA: Joni and Friends, 2010), n.p.
5. Joni Eareckson Tada and Steve Bundy with Pat Verbal, *Beyond Suffering*

Study Guide: A Christian View on Disability Ministry (Agoura Hills, CA: Joni and Friends, 2012), 45.

6. Susan Silk and Barry Goldman, "How Not to Say the Wrong Thing," *Los Angeles Times*, April 7, 2013, http://articles.latimes.com/2013/apr/07/opinion/la-oe-0407-silk-ring-theory-20130407.

7. Joni Eareckson Tada, "He Hears Our Cry," Joni and Friends Radio broadcast, June 3, 2011, http://www.joniandfriends.org/radio/1-minute/he-hears-our-cry/.

8. Kelli Ra Anderson, "Healing Prayers and Promises in Disability Parenting," *Not Alone* (blog), January 26, 2015, http://specialneedsparenting.net/healing-prayers-promises-disability-parenting/.

CHAPTER 20—BECOME A DISABILITY ADVOCATE

1. Jolene Philo, *Different Dream Parenting: A Practical Guide to Raising a Child with Special Needs* (Grand Rapids, MI: Discovery House, 2011), 19.

2. Jeff McNair, "People with Disabilities Need Advocates," *Disabled Christianity* (blog), June 6, 2004, http://disabledchristianity.blogspot.com/search?q=people+with+disabilities+need+advocates.

3. Ibid.

4. Shannon Dingle, "Four Challenges of Leading Disability Ministry as a Special Needs Parent," *Church4EveryChild* (blog), March 24, 2015, https://drgrcevich.wordpress.com/2015/03/24/four-challenges-of-leading-disability-ministry-as-a-special-needs-parent-shannon-dingle/.

5. Kathy Ostrowski, "Shock: Pediatricians Issue DNR to Minors Without Parental Permission," LifeNews.com, April 4, 2016, http://www.lifenews.com/2016/04/04/shock-pediatricians-issue-dnr-to-minors-without-parental-permission/.

6. Joni Eareckson Tada, "A Right to Die Update," Joni and Friends Radio broadcast, December 13, 2007, http://www.joniandfriends.org/radio/5-minute/right-die-update.

7. 1 Timothy 5:16.

8. "Join Us!—What to Expect," Jill's House, accessed May 31, 2017, http://jillshouse.org/plan-your-visit-what-to-expect.